The Jewish-American Kitchen

◆ ◆ ◆

The Jewish-American Kitchen

• • •

Raymond Sokolov

Recipes by Susan R. Friedland
Photographs by Louis Wallach

Stewart, Tabori & Chang

New York

FRONTISPIECE: *On Friday night, the Sabbath begins with roast chicken (page 60), noodle pudding (lokshen kugel, page 92), pickled beets (page 106), and challah (page 158), the braided loaf that is a symbol for this weekly day of rest. The lit candles stand for the first expression of the will of God at creation: "Let there be light." Their illumination traditionally begins the Sabbath, which commemorates the seventh and last day of creation, when God rested. Scripture does not specify a Sabbath menu, but this one has evolved as the post-Eden classic.*

Text and recipes copyright © 1989 Raymond Sokolov
Photographs copyright © 1989 Stewart, Tabori & Chang, Inc.

Published in 1989 by
Stewart, Tabori & Chang, Inc.
740 Broadway, New York, New York 10003

Library of Congress Cataloging-in-Publication Data

Sokolov, Raymond A.
    The Jewish-American kitchen / Raymond Sokolov; recipes by Susan R.
Friedland; photographs by Louis Wallach.
        p.   cm.
    Includes index.
    ISBN 1-55670-096-2 : $35.00
    1. Cookery, Jewish.   2. Cookery, American.   I. Friedland, Susan
R.   II. Title.
TX724.S63   1989   89-11321
641.5'676'0973—dc20   CIP

Distributed in the U.S. by Workman Publishing,
708 Broadway, New York, New York 10003
Distributed in Canada by Canadian Manda Group,
P.O. Box 920 Station U, Toronto, Ontario M8Z 5P9
Distributed in all other territories by Little,
Brown and Company, International Division,
34 Beacon Street, Boston, Massachusetts 02108

Printed in Japan
10 9 8 7 6 5 4 3 2 1

To the three Jo(e)s, Mike,
and the other Ray

◆   ◆   ◆

CONTENTS

◆   ◆   ◆

*An American-Jewish Sunday brunch in which everything but the tomato, the coffee,
and the newspaper hails from the Old Country, from the larder of Eastern Europe:
bagel, lox, cream cheese, onion.*

What is Jewish Food?

◆   ◆   ◆

What is Jewish food? It would be easier to answer that question if we knew, first of all, how to answer the fundamental question: What is a Jew? The rabbis have their answer, which is essentially the one adopted by the state of Israel for its Law of Return, which grants citizenship to anyone who can show that he or she is Jewish. In both cases, it boils down to having a Jewish mother. Hitler did not have so stringent an admissions requirement; all he insisted on was a single Jewish grandparent. Jean-Paul Sartre, somewhat influenced by his own wartime experience with the eagerness of anti-Semites to identify the largest number of people possible as Jews, argued that a Jew was anyone whom other people called a Jew. Finally, there is self-definition, the right of individual people to define themselves as Jews without certification from the outside, without reference to matrilineage, religious observance, or the opinion of others. Secular Jews, one might argue—and I certainly do—are Jews if they think of themselves as Jews. Perhaps it would even be more accurate, in this era of multiple roles and manifold identities, to say that secular Jews are Jews *when* they think of themselves as Jews.

So defining what is a Jew isn't really that hard. In a paragraph, you can state most of the important definitions. On the other hand, with Jewish food you may think you already know for sure what it is, but you won't be so confident after you've thought about it for a while. You can't really say, for instance, that Jewish food is what Jews eat (even assuming we've agreed we know what Jews are). Jews eat potatoes, frequently, all over the world. Religious Jews in long black kaftans, French Jews from North Africa in Yves Saint Laurent suits, and assimilated Jews in sports clothes in Hollywood taking lunch meetings at nouvelle cuisine restaurants with other assimilated tieless Jews in the movie business—they all eat potatoes. But so does the Pope, not to mention millions of his Irish faithful. No one in his right mind would call the potato a Jewish tuber. And yet....

And yet why not? The potato is always kosher, unless of course you fry it in lard or otherwise contaminate it, but I'm getting ahead of myself. For simplicity's sake, think of the potato all by itself. You could eat it in public for weeks, even years, and no one would say, "There, you see, he must be Jewish. Look at all the potatoes he eats." But if you did the same thing with bagels, cream cheese, and cured salmon....

All right, then, certain foods are marked as Jewish but a lot of things even orthodox Jews eat all the time are not marked as Jewish. This unmarked area is vast. Think of celery, tunafish, eggs, butter, Coca-Cola, radishes, coffee, yogurt, corn flakes, rainbow trout (I'm leaving out red meat here although most of it would qualify if it passed through the hands of a kosher butcher, and no one prevents non-Jews from buying meat from a kosher butcher). Jews eat almost everything, and they easily survived in the American Midwest, on a "gentile" diet of white bread, three veg, and fish back when they first arrived. But before long these pioneer communities began to find ways of supplying themselves with special Jewish foods. Kosherkeepers, of course, had to set up kosher butchering, but even the secular Jews were a market for specially marked Jewish foods, for bagels and lox, for matzo meal, and so on.

And, at the same time, they cooked dishes they thought of as theirs, but which historically and geographically first belonged to the cultures in which Jews have previously lived and adapted themselves to local conditions.

To take a distant example. Jews living in the Middle East eat many of the foods we in the West think of as Arab dishes. Hummus and falafel are, in fact, normal and habitual foods for Middle Eastern Jews, and this is why they are frequently seen in Jewish restaurants in Israel (not to mention in Israeli-style kosher restaurants in New York).

Similarly, Jews whose ancestors lived in Romania often eat a corn-meal mush they call mamaliga. This is really a Romanian dish with a Romanian name, but it was long ago assimilated into the Romanian-Jewish diet and therefore moved with Romanian Jews to other places, as did such Romanian dishes as pastrami and the garlic-laden sausages called carnatzlach.

Indeed, if we were to scrutinize the menus at most American-Jewish restaurants or in most American-Jewish homes, we would find that very few of the foods were, strictly speaking, Jewish and only Jewish. No raw material starts out as Jewish, not even chicken fat. No potato, no apple, no salmon is Jewish food per se. There are long lists of foods that are *not* Jewish, from shrimp cocktail to Szechuan pigs' ears, but in order to compile a list of strictly Jewish foods, we have to enter the kitchen and talk about food preparation, about recipes that are always associated with Jewish life and never with gentile life. This is a relatively small list, consisting mainly of dishes whose preparation grows directly out of the dietary laws and/or the exigencies of a particular holiday—matzo balls or cholent come to mind. The list could also be expanded a bit to include recipes borrowed from other cultures but changed to make them kosher.

But even this list would shortchange the Jewish kitchen. It would cut the heart out of the Jewish menu, which is a conglomeration of dishes borrowed from here and everywhere, dishes that have survived the trials of the Diaspora, dishes born of emigration and resettlement, and finally dishes that grow out of the creative assimilation of American ways.

I am speaking here of the American-Jewish menu, because a world-wide recipe book of foods eaten by Jews from Bokhara to Montevideo would be true in its way to modern Jewish life as a global phenomenon, but it would suffer from its very universalism. The book would strike no individual Jew as a record of his own experiences at table. In its cosmopolitanism, such a book would lose the specific flavors of Jewish food of any one place or time. Both gastronomically and intellectually, it would suffer from the same problems as "international" cooking always does. A complete Jewish cookbook would be authentic for no one.

Jewish cuisine is a meaningless notion unless it is tied to a time and a place. What is Jewish for Yemenite Jews is anthropology for us. And vice versa. By the same token, you don't have to be Jewish to like Jewish food. Millions of vegetarians all over the world eat a strictly kosher diet every day without even knowing it. But are they eating Jewish food? To say they are is to mock the dietary laws and the idea of Jewish food in general.

Simply because all fruits and vegetables are kosher does not make them Jewish. The purpose of kashruth, of the system of rules that define kosher food—food fit for Jews to eat—is to exclude non-Jews from Jewish tables and to force Jews to spend time together as Jews. Divorced from a Jewish context, a radish is only a radish. Chopped and served with sour cream to people thinking of themselves as Jews in this country, the same radish has acquired a Jewish resonance, even though the dish it comes as part of is a direct descendant of the general cuisine of Eastern Europe. The idea of mixing those locally common ingredients began there, as far as we know. Jews acquired the idea there and brought it with them here, and kept making it, although their gentile neighbors didn't. So when an American-Jewish family of Eastern European (Ashkenazic) heritage eats sour cream and radishes, they are eating what is for them Jewish food, marked as Jewish, whether they keep a kosher home or not, and even if they are all vegetarians. Conversely, an American ovo-lacto-vegetarian who heard about this dish and started eating it at home with the wild enthusiasm of a convert could not make the claim that he was eating Jewish food unless he had been taught it as a Jewish recipe. And even then, he would be a gastronomic tourist, as we all are when we cook "authentic" Julia Child-written French dishes—unless he took the trouble to experience the dish in a Jewish context and got some feel for the importance of "dairy" foods as a major part of Jewish culinary life.

In Jewish cooking, context is everything. What could a flourless Passover nut torte possibly mean to someone who had never been to a seder and who didn't understand the point of Passover baking, with its special restrictions? Yet even the most observant Jews can only feel the appropriate gastronomic resonance for foods they have experienced in a Jewish context themselves. Other Jewish food traditions are meaningless to them; at the most, they are appealingly exotic. Even the most authentically ancestral Jewish foods, the foods of the Old Testament, do not qualify as Jewish food for any living Jew, except in a distant historical way, as part of the antiquity of one's people, something like hieroglyphics for modern Egyptians.

Solomon (S.S. 8:2) sings of drinking "spiced wine of the juice of pomegranates," but who in all contemporary Ashkenazic Jewry has tasted this drink? And who today would want to prepare what may be the closest the Bible comes to a real recipe, Elisha's soup (2 Kings 4:38-42):

> *And Elisha came again to Gilgal: and there was a dearth in the land; and the sons of the prophets were sitting before him: and he said unto his servant, Set on the great pot, and seethe pottage for the sons of the prophets.*
>
> *And one went out into the field to gather herbs, and found a wild vine, and gathered thereof wild gourds his lap full, and came and shred them into the pot of pottage: for they knew them not.*
>
> *So they poured out for the men to eat. And it came to pass, as they were eating of the pottage, that they cried out, and said, O thou man of God, there is death in the pot. And they could not eat thereof.*

But he said, Then bring meal. And he cast it into the pot; and he said, Pour out for the people, that they may eat. And there was no harm in the pot.

And there came a man from Baal-shalisha, and brought the man of God bread of the first fruits, twenty loaves of barley, and full ears of corn in the husk thereof. And he said, Give unto the people, that they may eat.

Intrepid researchers have combed the Bible for such food references and then concocted recipes from them. It can be done, but it does not make a cuisine. The Talmudists found a richer pasture, explicating the ordinances of the law, which discuss food and how to deal with it at length but not in a way that suggests a specific cuisine, certainly not one anybody cooks today. In fact, the fullest discussions of food in the Torah, the Five Books of Moses that are the basis of Judaism, come in descriptions of sacrifice: a heifer's burnt skin and bones with the dung thrown in the fire for good measure. Blood spurts on the altar. This is not the world of any modern Jew's kitchen.

What we are is what we eat. And that is a special cuisine that has evolved here, in the United States. For most of us, this means a mixture of dishes, some marked as Jewish, some not. But most of the marked dishes, in most of our homes, are survivors from the wreckage of Ashkenazic Jewish life in Eastern Europe. Not all dishes eaten there have made it in this country. Gefilte miltz (stuffed spleen) is a curiosity. Lungen (lungs) are impossible to find. Who has eaten eiter (udder) in the last twenty years?

What remains is something new made from something old. Our grandmothers and mothers evolved it from the recipes and the way of life their mothers had practiced in urban ghettos and in those ragged hamlets called shtetlach. Out of their memory of that world, they created food that was like the old food, but food that was also feasible in America. They came from many corners of Europe and so does our cuisine, the one in this book.

◆ ◆ ◆

---◆---

Kashruth and Cookery

◆   ◆   ◆

*T*o cook Jewish food—even just to eat Jewish food—one must
come to grips with kashruth. "Kashruth" is the Hebrew noun
formed from the same root as the more familiar adjective,
kosher. "Kosher" means fit to eat. Kashruth is, therefore, the system of
determining such fitness.

Kashruth is no simple matter for those concerned to apply it with full
rigor. It has been called the most elaborate system of dietary regulation
ever worked out by any group of human beings. The Jewish preoccupa-
tion with food goes back to the very beginning of Jewish tradition. It
began in Eden with the forbidden fruit. The rest of the Old Testament
has provided subsequent rabbinical commentators with much informa-
tion, history, and prophecy about food and eating, which they considered and reconsidered during the ensuing centuries. And the process is
far from complete. The rise of chemical food additives has given experts
on kashruth a large new field of investigation. But over those same
centuries, millions of ordinary Jews, most of them housewives with
limited exposure to the Talmud, have carried forward the kosher ideal
with great energy, applying it everywhere in the world to the basic

human problem of getting dinner on the table. They have managed to do this because the Jewish dietary laws are mostly of straightforward application and can be explained to any reasonable adolescent in a few minutes.

Most of the complexity applies to meat—to the ritual slaughter of animals, to methods of inspecting their carcasses, and to the purification of meat for use in the kitchen. Few kosherkeepers worry much about any of this. They rely on a network of rabbinical inspectors, professional slaughterers or schochets, and on kosher butchers to make sure they are using kosher meat. Obviously non-kosher Jewish cooks can and do ignore all of this and buy meat wherever they please, although when they wish to cook in a Jewish mode, even these "cultural" Jews take care to purchase traditional cuts from animals not traditionally forbidden.

In other words, you cannot pretend to be preparing a Jewish meal even for emancipated Jews (or for non-Jews, come to think of it) if your menu begins with shrimp and moves on to pork roast. Jews never eat shellfish or pork, at least not when they are intending to eat as Jews. And so, whenever anybody wants to cook a Jewish meal, he or she must know the basic tenets of kashruth. Even for those who don't cook but only eat Jewish food, a knowledge of kashruth explains and deepens their appreciation of a cuisine so crucially determined by religious precept.

The late James Beard once published a recipe for Jewish corned beef sandwiches that advised spreading butter on the bread. Without thinking why, I felt so incensed at the idea that I attacked poor well-meaning Mr. Beard in print. Later, I realized that, although I had never lived in a kosher home, I had imbibed a kosherkeeper's revulsion for combinations of dairy foods and meat in Jewish dishes, of which, for me, the corned beef sandwich was pre-eminently one.

The kashruth primer that follows is no substitute for official rabbinical handbooks. Orthodox Jews in doubt on some point of practice will want to consult either their own rabbi or the Union of Orthodox Jewish

Congregations and Rabbinical Council of America's *Kashruth: Handbook for Home and School.* Conservative Jews can rely on the Rabbinical Assembly and the United Synagogue Commission on Jewish Education's *The Jewish Dietary Laws* by Samuel H. Dresner and David M. Pollock.

These books give clear explanations of the religious significance of kashruth and they give instructions on how to establish and maintain a kosher kitchen. They also attempt to elucidate the mysteries of Jewish butchering and of the "kashering" or final purification of meat through washing and salting to remove its blood. Since I am neither a rabbi nor a kosherkeeper, I wouldn't presume to advise anyone in these matters. But as a secular Jew with wide experience of Jewish food, I am going to summarize the basic ground rules of kashruth insofar as they affect the choice of ingredients, their combination, and the making of a Jewish menu. I do this to elucidate the religious background of the recipes in this book and to open an analytic window on Jewish cuisine for cooks and eaters.

What Types of Foods Are Kosher?   All fresh fruits and vegetables, unprocessed grains and cereals, milk and dairy products (except that cheese produced with animal rennet is forbidden in orthodox circles), eggs from kosher fowl (unless contaminated with specks of blood), all fish with fins and scales, meat of cud-chewing animals with cloven hooves (properly slaughtered, butchered, and purified), and most domestic fowl including chickens, ducks, turkeys, partridge, pheasant, quail, and peacock.

What Types of Foods Are Not Kosher (Treyf)?
Non–cud-chewing animals and those without cloven hooves, especially including pigs and rabbits; insects; predatory birds; amphibians; shellfish and catfish, eels, gars, lampreys, monkfish, sea squab, sharks, rays, skates, and, for some authorities, swordfish. Sturgeon also comes under suspicion because some people have doubted that it had true scales. Anyone concerned about such distinctions should seek rabbinical counsel.

The Kosher Kitchen   For the cook or eater, the main complexity in the kashruth system lies not so much in remembering which foods are forbidden and which are not. The real problem is to operate a kitchen without contaminating ingredients that are, in principle, perfectly kosher.

Milk and meat must be kept separate. All traditional Jewish cookery since the time of Moses has proscribed mixing meat and milk or milk products. This apparently straightforward but by now highly ramified and far-reaching tenet is based on Deuteronomy 14:21: "Thou shalt not seethe a kid in his mother's milk." After centuries of assiduous interpretation and reinterpretation of this simple-sounding idea, the whole of Jewish gastronomic life is divided into meat (flayshik) and dairy (milchik). The faithful begin by dividing their kitchens down the middle. They keep separate sets of dishes and pots and pans. To help them avoid mistakes, soap for dishwashing is sold in color-coded bars (red for meat, blue for dairy).

Not only must cooks avoid mixing meat and dairy products in the same dish or pot, but they must not mix meat and dairy dishes at the same meal. Steak with *maître d'hotel* butter is not kosher, obviously. But it is also forbidden to consume milk and meat foods at the same time even when the foods themselves don't come into physical contact with each other. You can't eat bread and butter side by side with chicken. Or, to put it more generally, whichever you eat first, milk or meat, determines what you can consume for the rest of the meal. In practice, whoever is planning the meal decides in advance whether it will be a meat or dairy meal and arranges the menu accordingly so that improper juxtapositions of foods do not occur on the same table.

Since the fundamental force of kashruth is to circumscribe the role of flesh in cuisine, the meat meal is a potent affair and what might be called its meatness stays in force even after diners get up from the table. Observant Jews wait as long as six hours after a meat meal before eating dairy foods again. Few people wait this long, but some interval is necessary. After a dairy meal, however, no wait (some people wait an hour) is required before it is permissible to eat meat again (unless the dairy meal included hard cheeses), but it is customary to signal the changeover, perhaps by changing the tablecloth.

In addition to milk foods and meat foods, there are pareve or neutral foods, which are neither meat nor milk and which can be served at any time. Pareve is, in fact, the largest category of foods and comprises vegetables, fruits, grains, fish, and eggs.

The Problem of Meat   Centuries of debate and discussion have contributed to the large literature and to the maze of regulations that surround the eating of meat in Jewish tradition. Without indulging in amateur Talmudism, it is still possible to relate the obsessional corpus of law on butchering and purification to three stages of quasi-historical development of attitudes on the subject that can be isolated in the text of Torah.

In the Garden of Eden, Adam and Eve are vegetarians. God bestows fruits and vegetables upon them, but nothing is said about meat or other animal foods.

The second stage comes after the expulsion from Paradise, in the world as we know it, where human beings who have descended into a compromised state kill their food. God told Noah and his sons (Genesis 9:3-4): "Every moving thing that liveth shall be meat for you; even as the green herb have I given you all things. But flesh with the life thereof, which is the blood thereof, shall ye not eat."

As a concession to human imperfection and worldly appetite, some commentators say, God allowed men to eat meat. And until the time of Moses, any meat was apparently permitted. But even at this stage a respect for animal life and a repugnance for animal blood restricted savage feasting on flesh. On the other hand, it is clear that pre-Mosaic biblical men did not keep kosher. The best evidence of this is that both Nimrod and Esau were hunters. Nimrod (Genesis 10:9) was "a mighty hunter before the Lord" and Esau (Genesis 27:3-4) hunted venison for his father Isaac because the old man wanted "savory meat" before he died. No modern observant Jew could eat meat procured with bow and arrow. Only meat from animals ritually slaughtered with a knife drawn swiftly through the neck arteries and esophagus, and butchered according to an elaborate set of rules, can be kosher today. But Nimrod and Esau lived before Moses received the laws recorded in Leviticus and Deuteronomy. So they were not bound in the way that later generations have been.

But once those laws were given to Moses by God, the process of interpreting them began, and it has evolved over centuries into a code of slaughter intended to cause the least possible suffering to kosher animals and to prevent the consumption of meat from blemished animals. Direct biblical prohibitions forbid eating animals that have "died of themselves" or had their flesh torn by other animals (the Hebrew for this is "terefah" from which we get the Yiddish term "treyf," which is now applied to all unacceptable meat). The primeval prohibition against blood continued even more emphatically.

In order to ensure that these principles are strictly observed, it is necessary to supervise slaughter and butchering from stem to stern. No hunter could inspect his prey in the field before he killed it to make sure it was without external blemish. He could hardly kill it in the correct manner. Nor would he likely possess the leisure or the learning to inspect the carcass internally. So even though deer are in principle kosher animals, cloven-hoofed ruminants, they can only be eaten if they are slaughtered like cattle, with a knife. For an observant Jew to eat wild venison, he or she would have to catch the animal alive and bring it unharmed to a proper abattoir, find a trained ritual butcher, and have him treat the deer as if it were a lamb.

The most intricate part of kosher meat procurement comes after the actual slaughter, when the carcass is inspected for internal blemishes and forbidden adhesions. The early rabbinic writing on these matters was based on such close observation of animal organs that those treatises are now important documents in the history of animal anatomy. Anyone interested in taking a look at the standard modern compilation should consult *The Kosher Code of the Orthodox Jew* (New York: Sepher-Hermon Press, 1975). This is an obscure and technical book, full of passages like: "If the roof of the crop is perforated through, by a hole of any sort, the animal is terefah. What is its roof? It is that part which is dragged up into sight by the gullet when the fowl stretches its neck. But when the rest of the crop is perforated, the animal is permitted."

Perhaps the most crucial of the anatomical regulations comes directly out of the Bible. When Jacob wrestled with the angel, the angel touched him upon the hollow of his thigh and left it out of joint. "Therefore the children of Israel eat not of the sinew which shrank, which is upon the hollow of the thigh"(Genesis 32:32). The "sinew" is the sciatic nerve. It must be removed from an animal's hindquarters before the meat can be eaten. Ashkenazic authorities ruled that butchers were incompetent to do this, so they outlawed meat from the hindquarters altogether, thereby eliminating sirloin steak and (hindquarter) leg of lamb from the kosher larder. This prohibition is not observed in Sephardic communities and in Israel, where specialists called menakrim are trusted to remove the sciatic nerve and render hindquarters kosher.

After successfully inspected meat leaves the slaughterhouse, it must then be kashered to remove the blood. This can be done by broiling on a rack or by elaborate soaking and salting with Kosher salt (coarse enough not to melt right away as table salt would, but not so coarse that it rolls off the meat). Liver, because it contains a great deal of blood, can only be kashered by broiling.

The Sabbath

The general prohibition against work on the Jewish Sabbath (which runs from sundown Friday until Saturday evening) includes cooking. Warming is, however, allowed if 1) the source of heat was kindled before the beginning of the Sabbath, covered with a special tin plate or blech, and not adjusted once it has been lit; 2) the food to be reheated must have been previously cooked; and 3) liquids must not be brought to a boil. This greatly restricts the Sabbath diet. Even the Friday night meal must be set to cooking in the afternoon, before sundown. There are no set dishes for this evening meal, except for the braided bread called challah. On Saturday, the main Sabbath meal is lunch—after the all-morning synagogue service and before nightfall, when the Sabbath and its culinary restrictions end. But these very restrictions have given rise to a special form of hot food called cholent in Ashkenazic homes. Cholent actually goes by many other names and is eaten in many forms the world over. It is the most diverse and intellectually interesting of all Jewish foods.

An Excursus on Cholent
In this country, with its overwhelming Ashkenazic coloration, cholent is almost always a slow-cooked stew of beans and beef called cholent. I once heard the poet John Hollander refer to cholent as the cassoulet of the Jews, which was an apt description, given the narrow definition that contemporary American-Jewish usage gives to cholent. The mistake most of us make— I certainly did until very recently—is to think of cholent as a dish. It is in fact the Eastern Yiddish term for a category of Sabbath dishes eaten originally in Ashkenazic Europe. The meat-and-bean cholent we think of as standard substituted potatoes for beans in Russia. And there are richer variations that combine meat (including calves feet in a Galician variant) with beans, potato, and barley. A cholent could just as well be a pudding of baked grated potato or noodles known generically in Yiddish as kugel. In Bavaria kugels even included apples and matzo.

So a cholent was not always a cholent. In fact, throughout the western range of Yiddish speech, from Germany to France, it wasn't even called a cholent; the word schalet was in use instead. Schalet even found its way into the standard encyclopedia of French gastronomy, *Larousse Gastronomique*, as *schalet à la Juive*, which turns out to be a double-crusted applesauce pie.

The German-Jewish poet Heinrich Heine rhapsodized about schalet in one of his "Hebrew Melodies," a ballad called "Princess Sabbath" ("Prinzessin Sabbat") that overtly parodies Schiller's "Ode to Joy," the text Beethoven used for his Ninth Symphony:

Schalet, schöner Götterfunken,
Tochter aus Elysium!
Also klänge Schillers Hochlied
Hätt' er Schalet je gekostet.

Schalet ist die Himmelspeise
Die der liebe Herrgott selber
Einst den Moses kochen lehrte
Auf dem Berge Sinai. . . .

Schalet ist des wahren Gottes
Koscheres Ambrosia. . . .

(Cholent, spark struck from God, daughter of Elysium!
That's how Schiller would have sung his ode if he had ever
tasted cholent. Cholent is the food of heaven, which the
Lord God himself once taught Moses to cook on Mt.
Sinai. . . . Cholent is the kosher ambrosia of the true
God. . . .)

The comparison is bombastic but apt in one way at least: neither ambrosia nor cholent is a definable food in the ordinary sense. We can't write a recipe for either one. Ambrosia is celestial food in the abstract; cholent is any hot food that satisfies the religious definition of a dish kosher for shabbat (Sabbath).

Work is prohibited on the Sabbath. This means that the lighting of fires is forbidden, as is cooking in most senses of the word. It would, of course, be possible to satisfy these basic conditions by eating cold leftovers, so long as they were normally kosher. But the Sabbath is not meant as a day of suffering, so special efforts are made to serve hot food whose preparation does not involve cooking or lighting fires.

The Sabbath begins at sundown on Friday, which means that the Friday evening meal is not particularly difficult to bring off in accordance with the sabbath rules. The Jewish wife gets her meal underway in the afternoon and plans it so that her work for it ends before dark. The problem meal is Saturday lunch. The solution is a filling one-pot dish whose prep work can be completed before sundown on Friday. From there on, for the ensuing 16 to 20 hours, the covered dish cooks slowly, in an oven or on top of the stove over an asbestos pad or other heat-diminishing device (the Yiddish name for this is blech, for tin or sheet metal).

Strict observers don't remove the pot cover to see how their cholent is doing, nor do they stir it or add water or in any active way cook the dish. And when they get around to serving it, they can only return it to the oven or the blech if 1) it was their intention to do so when they removed it, and 2) they did not set it down anywhere else while they were serving it. These restrictions may not be observed except by the most zealous householders, but they derive coherently from a liturgical phrase in the Talmud that is repeated in the synagogue service on Friday night. This Mishnah or rabbinical commentary, first introduced into the liturgy in Babylon in the ninth century, deals with preparations for the Sabbath and in particular the question of kindling fires. It contains a phrase (*taman et hakhamin*) that translates literally as "hide or bury the hot things," meaning cover the hot food.

As Paul Wexler and others have shown, the two basic words of this phrase have impressed themselves on all the Jewish languages of the Diaspora, from the Judeo-Arabic of Yemen to the Yiddish of Vilna to the transplanted Baghdadi Arabic of Calcutta. The actual dishes vary from place to place quite radically, but their mode of cooking remains roughly the same, and their names are words that translate the original Hebrew-Aramaic words meaning hidden or hot:

Many false etymologies for cholent have been put forward. The most ingenious is Shul Ende, the end of the synagogue (service). Another derives it from the French word for shallot, *echalote*. A third connects it with a Hebrew expression implying "kept in the oven." But the word clearly emerges out of Vulgar Latin *calente*(m) or some early Romance form of the word for hot (later yielding Spanish *caliente*, Catalan *calent*, and French *chaud*, from Old French *chauld*). The Hebrew-Aramaic hot-word *khamin* is itself used as the name for Sabbath food in some Arabized settings, and in Calcutta, it crops up as *hameen*. But the other key Mishnaic notion, hidden, shows itself all over the Middle East in various forms of the same basic Arabic root (*dfina, tfina, adafina, adefina*) all meaning covered or buried. In Iraq, some speakers substituted yet other synonyms for covered: *tbit* (<spend the night<take shelter) and *kubanah* (a sabbath food made of millet, apparently related to a verb meaning hem or conceal); and in Yemen, Judeo-Arabic has *gillah* (Sabbath bean dish <earthen jug).

In Spain, what I am going to call the cholent concept produced that most typical of Madrid dishes, the boiled dinner with chickpeas known to the wide world as *cocido madrileno*, but still referred to by Spanish Jews as adafina. In its pure form, this dish contained no pork, but supposedly after the expulsion of the Jews from Spain in 1492, the nominally converted marranos who managed to stay behind added pork to show their fealty to their new faith. Some of the refugees or their descendants must have come to the Americas. No doubt some of them did bring traditional Sabbath food ideas with them. Somewhere, then, perhaps even before 1500, some European Jew must have cooked dfina in the New World, spreading the planet's most cosmopolitan food idea to yet another continent. Perhaps there should be a monument to this un-known dfina erected on Puerto Rico or some other site of early Spanish penetration.

The dfina that Claudia Roden grew up with in Egypt (and published a recipe for in *A Book of Middle Eastern Food*) is a very close relative of the cocido, but it contains the unshelled eggs known as hamine. Long slow cooking turns their insides creamy and colors their shells brown. Léone Jaffin prints several Algerian variants of dfina in *150 recettes et mille et un souvenirs d'une juive d'Algérie*. One version adds Swiss chard to the traditional meat and chickpea stew. Another substitutes dried favas for the chickpeas. A third substitutes bulgur wheat and a fourth adds a pasta in the shape of coffee beans.

After Algerian independence, adafina came to metropolitan France with the *pieds noirs* Jewish refugees. And, according to Norman Stillman, a specialist in the history of Jews in Arab countries, French-speaking Jews today shorten adafina to daf, as in *J'ai mangé un bon daf*.

In Morocco, the same basic dish is also known as sefrina (or skhina), meaning hot. But the most exotic "hot" cholent is the hameen of Calcutta, which accommodates to local taste by adding typical Indian spices and substituting chicken for the beef repugnant to the Hindu majority. Rice replaces chickpeas.

The cynic might wonder out loud if this transplanted Iraqi stew hasn't been converted in every way but name into a chicken curry. Similarly, all of the cholents from hither and yon could be subsumed under the heading *pot-au-feu* or *olla podrida*. A daf by any other name. . . .

But that misses the point. The name for once really does define the dish. A cholent is a dfina is a hameen, all of them hot and buried, cooked while you sleep and pray. The concept transmogrifies the ingredients, whatever they may start out as, into kosher ambrosia.

◆   ◆   ◆

CHAPTER

I

Appetizers

◆   ◆   ◆

Egg salad with onion and gribenes (page 28).

SHMALTZ

Since the kosher laws don't permit the use of dairy fat (butter) with meat, Jews not living in places with easy access to vegetable or olive oil turned to chickens. They produced their own flavorful meat-cooking fat by purifying chicken fat and storing it until needed. The solid matter is not discarded but treasured as gribenes and eaten immediately or, in kitchens run by generous cooks, added to mashed potatoes.

The richest deposit of chicken fat appears in the neck of a raw chicken. One chicken will not yield enough raw fat to be worth rendering; a fowl will give up barely enough. Harbor chicken fat in the freezer. When you have a substantial quantity, render it, as indicated below. The rendered fat also keeps well in the freezer.

◆　　　◆　　　◆

6 ounces chicken fat
3 ounces chicken skin, shredded
1 large onion, peeled, and sliced thin

In a heavy skillet, combine the fat with the chicken skin and the onion. Cook slowly for about 45 minutes. The undissolved bits of fat, the skin, and the onion should be golden and tempting. Strain the fat through washed cheesecloth. The gribenes will remain in the cheesecloth. *Makes 1 cup.*

EGGS AND ONIONS APPETIZER

Although the gribenes are listed here as optional, I urge you to include them. Gribenes are cracklings, the irresistible brown and crunchy solids that appear magically when chicken fat is rendered.

◆　　　◆　　　◆

6 hard-boiled eggs, quartered
1/2 cup minced onions or scallions
1 tablespoon gribenes (optional, see preceding recipe)
Salt
Freshly ground black pepper
3 tablespoons shmaltz

Chop the eggs (don't mash them) and add the onions or scallions and the gribenes. Chop until well blended.

Add salt, pepper, and the shmaltz. Continue chopping just to combine. Serve at room temperature with matzos, black bread, or challah. *Makes 2 cups.*

MUSHROOMS, EGGS, AND ONIONS

2 tablespoons shmaltz or margarine
1/3 cup minced onions
1 cup minced mushrooms (1/4 pound)
4 hard-boiled eggs, chopped
Salt
Freshly ground black pepper

Heat the shmaltz or margarine in a skillet and slowly cook the onions until soft but not brown. Add the mushrooms and cook slowly until the liquid given off by the mushrooms evaporates.

Combine the hard-boiled eggs and the mushroom-onion mixture on a large board. Mix and chop simultaneously until the mixture is almost pastelike. Season with salt and pepper. Scrape the mixture into a serving bowl, cover, and chill for a few hours. Serve with crackers, toast, matzos, or bread. *Makes 1 1/2 cups.*

EGGPLANT APPETIZER

*I*f chopped liver is the foie gras of the Jews, then this vigorously flavored eggplant purée is our caviar. The dish, variously seasoned, is a standard feature of cuisines from Greece to Baku. Without the egg garnish, it can begin a meat meal as well as a dairy, but the sieved egg garnish completes the caviar conceit.

◆　　◆　　◆

1 medium eggplant (1 1/4 to 1 1/2 pounds)
1/2 cup chopped onions
2 teaspoons minced garlic
3 tablespoons olive oil
1 tablespoon lemon juice
Salt
Freshly ground black pepper
1 hard-boiled egg

Preheat the oven to 400 degrees.

Cut off and discard the green cap of the eggplant. Pierce the eggplant in several places with a fork, and bake it in a shallow pan until tender, about 45 minutes.

Slice the eggplant in half lengthwise and scoop out the flesh. Add the onions and garlic and chop until the mixture is well combined and finely minced, but not a smooth purée. Add the olive oil and lemon juice. Mix well and season with salt and pepper to taste.

Transfer the mixture to a serving bowl and refrigerate, covered, for at least 1 hour. The eggplant will keep for several days.

Before serving, sieve the hard-boiled egg over the top of the eggplant. *Makes 2 cups.*

OVERLEAF: *Golden rich gribenes emerge from rendered (melted) shmaltz (chicken fat). A rich snack for those who know where to find it.*

KNISHES

*K*nishes are an ideal cocktail snack, so perfect in fact that it is hard to believe that they were invented before the cocktail. Knishes are simple stuffed pastries, like their cousins, Russian pirozhki. As is shown below, they can be made from a pastry dough or a potato dough and stuffed with kasha (buckwheat groats) or mashed potatoes.

◆　　◆　　◆

Potato Dough Knishes

1 cup mashed potatoes (peeled, boiled, and put
　through a ricer, or mashed dry with a fork)
3 eggs, lightly beaten
3 cups all-purpose flour, plus additional for
　rolling
Salt
1 egg yolk, lightly beaten with 1 tablespoon
　water

Combine the mashed potatoes and eggs. Sift in the flour and salt. Beat with an electric mixer or a wooden spoon until the dough is smooth.

Preheat the oven to 350 degrees.

Divide the dough in thirds. On a lightly floured board, roll out one piece of the dough into a 10-inch square. With a scant cup of filling (see recipes that follow), make a mound on the dough about 7 inches long, 3 inches wide. Roll into a rectangle about 8 x 3 inches, tucking in the ends. Place, seams down, on an oiled baking sheet. Repeat with the rest of the dough. Brush with the egg yolk and bake for 40 to 45 minutes. The pastry will probably split in baking. Slice into 1 to 1 1/2-inch pieces and serve. *Makes 18-24 slices.*

Pastry Dough Knishes

*2 cups all-purpose flour, plus additional for
    kneading and rolling*
1 teaspoon baking powder
1/2 teaspoon salt
1 to 2 tablespoons oil
2 eggs, lightly beaten

Mix together the flour, baking powder, and
salt in the bowl of a standing electric mixer
fitted with a dough hook. Add 1 tablespoon
of the oil, the eggs, and 2 tablespoons water.
Knead for 3 or 4 minutes, adding the remaining oil and water if necessary to make a
smooth dough. Alternatively, combine the
dry ingredients in a large bowl. Make a well
in the center and add the oil, eggs, and
water. Mix well with a wooden spoon until
smooth. Knead on a floured board for 5 or 6
minutes.

Place the dough in an oiled bowl, cover
with a dishtowel, and let stand for 1 hour.

Meanwhile, preheat the oven to 350
degrees.

Divide the dough in thirds. On a floured
surface, roll one piece of the dough into a
thin rectangle, about 10 or 11 inches long.
Mound 2/3 to 3/4 cup of filling (see the
recipes that follow) along the long end,
about 1 inch high. Roll up like a jelly roll
and pinch the ends together. Repeat with
the rest of the dough. For large, individual
knishes, roll out the dough and cut rectan-
gles about 9 by 5 inches. Fill the center of
each rectangle with about 3 tablespoons of
filling and fold over the ends of the dough,
one after the other. Pinch all the edges
closed. Bake the knishes for about 40 minutes, until brown. Slice and serve. *Makes
about 2 dozen slices or 1 dozen large
knishes.*

Kasha Filling

2 tablespoons shmaltz
1 cup chopped onions
3 cups cooked kasha (see page 97)
1 egg, lightly beaten
Salt
Freshly ground black pepper

Heat the shmaltz in a small skillet and add
the onions. Sauté until soft and lightly colored. Remove from the heat and combine
with the kasha. Add the egg and season with
salt and pepper to taste.

Potato Filling

1/4 cup shmaltz or oil
3 cups minced onions
*3 cups mashed potatoes (peeled, boiled, and put
    through a ricer, or mashed with a fork)*
Salt
Freshly ground black pepper

Heat the shmaltz or oil in a medium skillet.
Add the onions and sauté until soft and
lightly colored. Remove from the heat and
combine with the potatoes. Season with salt
and pepper—the mixture will need a lot of
both.

LEFT: *A pastry dough for the individual knish (page 33) and potato dough for the roll (page 32). Both are stuffed with mashed potatoes (page 33). Slice thin, but not too thin.*

ABOVE: *One of the mainstays of the Jewish-American delicatessen: chopped liver (page 37) with dark pumpernickel. Hold the butter.*

P'TCHA

Perhaps p'tcha is an acquired taste. It is true that few of us anymore grow up being served calves' foot jelly as an hors d'oeuvre. But once most people have tasted p'tcha, they see the light, for here is a delicate and cooling start to a meat meal.

◆　　◆　　◆

2 calves' feet, quartered
2 onions, peeled and quartered
3 carrots, halved lengthwise
8 to 10 parsley sprigs
6 hard-boiled eggs
2 tablespoons minced garlic

Wash the calves' feet well and place them in a large, heavy saucepan with the onions, carrots, and parsley. Cover with 2 1/2 to 3 quarts cold water. The vegetables and the calves' feet should be totally covered, but don't use a pot so large that more than 3 quarts of water will be necessary.

Bring to a boil and skim the foam that rises to the surface. Lower the heat, cover the pan, and simmer, skimming from time to time, for 3 to 4 hours, until the bones easily separate from the meat and cartilage.

Strain the broth through a fine sieve lined with cheesecloth directly into a large bowl. Remove and discard the bones and vegetables.

Mash 2 of the hard-boiled egg yolks and combine with a cup or so of the broth. Pour this mixture back into the large bowl of broth. This will give the finished jelly a more appealing color.

Chop the meat and cartilage and combine with the minced garlic. Slice the remaining hard-boiled eggs, including the two extra whites. Spread the meat in a small roasting pan or two 8-inch square pans; cover with the sliced eggs. After it's cooled a bit, strain the broth through a fine sieve over the meat and refrigerate, uncovered, until it starts to set. Remove the solidified layer of fat on the surface. Cover with plastic wrap and chill for at least 12 hours or until completely set. Before serving, cut in squares. *Makes 10 to 15 appetizer servings.*

CHOPPED LIVER

This is the epitome of Jewish cooking as we know it in this country—rich but simple, elegantly smooth but not at all fancy-shmancy. This is a Jewish liver mousse because all its ingredients are kosher and it uses an animal fat—shmaltz, rendered chicken fat—as a liaison for the livers—not and never butter. And no cream either. That would be French (*gateau de foies blonds de volaille*), but it would also be treyf and would taste entirely different. Onions give this spread its other main taste. Thorough but not complete puréeing gives chopped liver a homemade texture. It works well as a cocktail spread, in sandwiches, or on lettuce as a first course.

◆   ◆   ◆

2 to 4 tablespoons shmaltz
1 pound chicken livers
4 medium onions (about 1 pound), peeled and
　　chopped
2 hard-boiled eggs
Salt
Freshly ground black pepper

Melt 1 tablespoon of the shmaltz in a heavy skillet over medium heat. Add the chicken livers in batches and cook thoroughly until no trace of pink remains. Alternatively, broil the livers until cooked through. Cool.

Add 1 tablespoon shmaltz and the onions to the skillet and cook over low heat until soft but not brown. A nontraditional but very good method is to cook only half of the onions and add the remaining raw onions, finely minced, to the cooked livers.

Put the livers, onions, and the hard-boiled eggs through the coarse blade of a meat grinder. Alternatively, chop the livers and onions in a processor, using a few very short pulses—be careful not to make a paste. Then finely chop the eggs separately and add by hand.

Season the mixture with salt and pepper—it will need substantial quantities of both. Add an additional tablespoon or two of shmaltz if the spread seems too dry. *Makes about 3 cups.*

Soups

◆ ◆ ◆

Potatoes ''beef'' up this hot beet borscht (page 41).

BORSCHT

*I*n its simplest form, beet borscht is merely a cold soup made from beets and their cooking liquid.

There are, however, many more borschts than the familiar cold soup everyone knows. The variations given here are all more substantial meat dishes that could easily serve as main dishes for a winter lunch, accompanied by plenty of rye bread. The Cabbage and Meat Borscht has no beets at all.

◆   ◆   ◆

COLD BEET BORSCHT

2 pounds beets (8 to 10 medium), washed and
   trimmed
Salt
Sugar
1 tablespoon lemon juice
2 boiled potatoes, peeled and halved (optional)
2 hard-boiled eggs, chopped (optional)
2 scallions, trimmed and chopped (optional)
1 cucumber, peeled and chopped (optional)

Cover the beets with lightly salted water and bring to a boil. Lower heat and simmer, uncovered, until the beets are tender.

Remove beets from liquid. As soon as you can handle them, rub off the outer skin and trim away any remaining pieces of root and stem. Dice, grate, or julienne the beets and return them to their cooking liquid. Chill.

When ready to serve, add lemon juice and sugar to taste (sugar is traditional but eliminate it if you are happy with unsugared borscht).

Garnish with potato, chopped eggs, scallion, or cucumber, if you wish.

Serve chilled. Pass sour cream so that it can be dolloped on the borscht liberally.
Makes 4 servings.

Hot Beet Borscht

3 pounds flanken
1 onion, peeled and chopped
1 small parsley root, peeled and chopped (about
    1/2 cup)
1 small celery root, peeled and chopped (about
    1 cup)
2 garlic cloves, peeled and halved
2 carrots, peeled and chopped
1/2 teaspoon caraway seeds
Salt
Freshly ground black pepper
2 pounds beets (8 to 10 medium), peeled and
    cut into julienne strips
1 tablespoon lemon juice
3 tablespoons sugar
1 to 2 pounds potatoes, peeled and boiled

Cover the flanken with 2 quarts of water in a heavy 6-quart pot and bring to a boil. Skim the foam as it rises to the surface. Add the onion, parsley root, celery root, garlic, carrots, caraway seeds, and salt and pepper. Cover partially and simmer for 1 hour.

In a saucepan, cover the beets with 1 quart of water and bring to a simmer with the lemon juice and sugar. Cover and simmer for 30 minutes.

Drain the flanken in a colander set over a large bowl. Chop the meat into bite-size pieces. Discard the vegetables. Skim and discard any fat from the surface of the cooking liquid.

Wipe out the large pot and pour in the strained cooking liquid and the chopped flanken. Add the beets and the liquid in which they cooked. Taste for seasoning. Simmer the borscht, partially covered, for an additional hour, until the meat is very tender. Skim any fat from the surface and serve with boiled potatoes. *Makes 6 to 8 servings.*

Meat and Vegetable Borscht

3 pounds flanken
2 onions, peeled and chopped
1/2 small celery root, peeled and chopped (about
    1 cup)
1/2 small green cabbage, shredded (about
    4 cups)
1 1/2 pounds beets (6 to 8 medium), peeled and
    chopped
1 small parsley root, peeled and chopped (about
    1/2 cup)
2 tablespoons lemon juice
Salt
Freshly ground black pepper
1 bay leaf
1 tablespoon brown sugar

Cover the flanken with 2 quarts of water in a heavy 6-quart pot and bring to a boil. Skim the foam as it rises to the surface. Reduce the heat and add the vegetables, lemon juice, salt, pepper, bay leaf, and brown sugar. Simmer for about 1 1/2 hours, until the meat is tender.

Slice the meat from the bones, discarding any fat and gristle. Reserve the meat. Strain the soup into a bowl, and if you have the time, put it in the refrigerator so the fat will harden for easy removal. Discard the vegetables. If you want to serve the soup immediately, skim off as much fat as you can with a large metal spoon. Return the meat to the broth, heat through, and serve. *Makes 6 to 8 servings.*

Cabbage and Meat Borscht

*T*his soup is best made a day in advance of serving. The fat is easily removed from the top after the soup has been refrigerated, and the flavors develop with some sitting time.

◆　　　◆　　　◆

1 or 2 marrow or knuckle bones
3 pounds flanken
2 cups chopped onions
2 garlic cloves, peeled and crushed
1 green cabbage (2 1/2 to 3 pounds), cored and shredded (about 12 cups)
1 tablespoon caraway seeds
2 teaspoons salt
Freshly ground black pepper
3 tablespoons lemon juice
1 tablespoon sugar

Put the bones and flanken in a 5- to 6-quart soup pot, cover with 3 quarts of cold water, and bring to a boil. Lower the heat and skim any foam as it rises to the surface. Simmer for 15 to 20 minutes, skimming.

Add the onions, garlic, cabbage, caraway seeds, salt, and pepper. Stir to combine. Cover the pot and simmer for 2 hours.

Remove the flanken and marrow bones and continue simmering the soup. Slice the meat off the flanken bones, discarding the fat and gristle. Put the meat back in the pot. Add the lemon juice and sugar and simmer for another 30 minutes. If you plan to eat the soup immediately, skim as much fat as you can from the surface with a large flat spoon. If you can wait, strain the soup and refrigerate the liquid and solids separately. After 8 hours or so, the fat will harden and can be removed easily. Recombine the broth and solids and bring to a simmer before serving. Season the soup with additional salt, lemon juice, and/or sugar, to taste. *Makes 8 to 10 servings.*

Vegetable Soup with Meat

*H*ere is another serious soup that embellishes its basic strengths—homemade stock, powerfully flavored dried mushrooms, chickpeas, and kidney beans—with six varieties of fresh vegetables.

◆　　　◆　　　◆

1/4 cup dried chickpeas
1/4 cup dried red kidney beans
1/2 ounce dried Polish or porcini mushrooms
1 cup chopped onions
1 tablespoon minced garlic
6 cups beef stock (see page 49)
2 cups cubed meat from the stock
3 carrots, scraped and sliced into rounds
1 zucchini, scrubbed, cubed, and quartered
1 broccoli stalk, cut into florets, stem peeled and cubed
1/4 pound green beans, halved
1/4 pound fresh mushrooms, quartered
1/2 cup shelled peas

Soak the chickpeas and kidney beans separately in water to cover overnight.

Soak the dried mushrooms for 30 minutes in 1 cup of boiling water. Strain through a fine sieve lined with paper towels or cheesecloth. Remove the mushrooms (leaving dirt and grit in the sieve) and chop them coarsely. Reserve the liquid.

In a heavy 6-quart pot, bring the drained chickpeas, kidney beans, onions, dried mushrooms and their reserved liquid, garlic, and beef stock to a boil. Reduce the heat, partially cover the pot, and simmer for 1 hour.

Add the meat and all the prepared vegetables except the peas, and cook for 30 minutes. Add the peas for the last 5 minutes of cooking. *Makes 6 to 8 servings.*

Take these ingredients, follow Aunt Mary Friedland's recipe and, presto change-o, you have vegetable soup with meat.

LENTIL SOUP WITH FRANKFURTERS

8 cups beef stock (see page 49)
1 cup chopped carrots
1 cup chopped celery and a few celery leaves
2 cups chopped onions
2 cups lentils, rinsed
1 bay leaf
Salt
Freshly ground black pepper
2 tablespoons shmaltz
1 1/2 pounds knockwurst or frankfurters, cut
    into 1/2-inch pieces

Combine the broth, carrots, celery and celery leaves, 1 cup of the chopped onions, the lentils, bay leaf, salt, and pepper in a large saucepan. Simmer, partially covered, for 30 minutes.

Slowly cook the remaining onions until soft in the shmaltz. Add to the soup along with the knockwurst or frankfurters and cook for another 20 to 30 minutes. Discard the bay and celery leaves, season to taste with salt and pepper, and serve. *Makes 8 servings.*

SPLIT PEA SOUP

*P*lease note that this soup is *not* flavored with a ham bone. The flanken transposes it into a darker key, changes it from a tenor into a baritone, so to speak.

◆   ◆   ◆

2 cups split peas
2 1/2 to 3 pounds flanken
Knuckle bones (optional)
Salt
2 carrots, chopped
1 celery stalk, chopped
1 onion or leek, peeled and chopped
3 parsley sprigs
Freshly ground black pepper

Place the split peas, flanken, and bones (if you are using them) in a 4-quart saucepan. Cover with 8 to 10 cups of cold water and add a pinch of salt. Bring to a boil. Reduce the heat, partially cover, and simmer for 30 minutes, skimming as needed.

Add the vegetables, parsley, and salt and pepper. Partially cover the pan and simmer for an additional 1 1/2 to 2 hours, until the meat is tender.

Remove and discard the parsley sprigs and the knuckle bones if you used them. Set aside the flanken. Purée the split peas and vegetables with the cooling liquid in a food mill or processor. Cut the meat off the flanken bones, discarding any fat and gristle. Cut the meat into bite-size pieces and return to the puréed soup. Reheat and serve. If the soup seems too thick, add more water. *Makes 6 servings.*

POTATO SOUP

*D*on't leave out the caraway seeds. They elevate an already excellent potato soup to a higher plane.

◆　　　◆　　　◆

3 tablespoons butter, margarine, or oil
3 cups chopped onions
3 pounds small red potatoes, washed and
*   quartered, or all-purpose potatoes, peeled*
*   and cubed*
1/2 cup chopped celery
1 cup diced carrots
1 teaspoon caraway seeds
Salt
Freshly ground black pepper
2 tablespoons farina
3 cups milk or water
1/2 cup chopped parsley

Heat the butter, margarine, or oil in a large soup pot. Add the onions and cook over low heat until softened, about 10 minutes.

Add the potatoes, celery, carrots, caraway seeds, salt, pepper, and 4 cups of water; the vegetables should be barely covered. Bring to a boil. Stir in the farina, cover partially, and simmer for 20 minutes. Stir in the milk or water and continue to simmer for 10 to 15 minutes, until the potatoes are tender but not falling apart. Just before serving, stir in the parsley. Pass sour cream separately. *Makes 6 to 8 servings.*

MUSHROOM-BARLEY SOUP

*T*his was my favorite soup as a child. It can be made with ordinary fresh mushrooms, but the dried ones recommended here bring a whiff of deep forest to every bowl. It is simple to make, easy to keep around, and excellent for serving to vegetarians.

◆　　　◆　　　◆

1 ounce dried porcini or Polish mushrooms
1 to 1 1/2 cups minced onions
1 cup minced carrots
1 cup minced celery
1 cup pearl barley
Salt
Freshly ground black pepper

Soak the dried mushrooms in 1 cup of boiling water for 30 to 60 minutes.

Meanwhile, put the onions, carrots, and celery in a 6-quart pot with the barley and 10 cups of cold water. Bring to a boil, reduce the heat, and begin to simmer.

Strain the dried mushrooms through a fine sieve lined with paper towels or cheesecloth. Pour the liquid (now about 1/2 cup) into the soup pot. Remove the mushrooms (leaving any grit or sand in the sieve) and coarsely chop them. Add to the soup pot.

Simmer the soup, partially covered, for about 45 minutes, or until the barley is tender. Season with salt and pepper to taste and serve with fresh snipped dill. *Makes 8 to 10 servings.*

Note: the longer the soup sits, the more liquid will be absorbed by the barley. So, if the soup is reheated, add more water.

OVERLEAF: *In sickness or in health, the chicken soup (page 48) in preparation here will make you feel much better about life. The kreplach (page 52), stuffed triangular pastries for the soup, will make you feel better still. Remember to pinch the points of the kreplach together.*

CHICKEN SOUP

*T*his is a very rich and delicious chicken soup. You will get a good soup using only one fowl, but the flavor will have less depth. Either version cures all illnesses. With two fowls, it works twice as fast.

◆　　　◆　　　◆

One 5- to 6-pound fowl (older chicken), including neck and giblets but without the liver

2 large onions, halved but unpeeled

3 carrots, scraped and cut into large chunks

10 to 15 parsley sprigs

18 to 20 black peppercorns, crushed

Remove the fat from the cavities of the fowl and set aside for rendering for future use.

Place the fowl in a stockpot with 5 or 6 quarts of cold water and the vegetables. The vegetables and fowl should be barely covered with water. Bring to a boil and immediately lower the heat. Skim any foam that rises to the surface and adjust the heat so just the odd bubble appears on the surface. Add the peppercorns, partially cover the pot, and simmer for about 2 hours, skimming occasionally. The fowl should be cooked through but not falling apart.

Remove the fowl to a large platter and when it is cool enough to handle, remove the meat from the bones. Reserve the meat for sandwiches or salad or kreplach filling (see page 52). Return the bones and skin to the simmering soup and cook for another hour or so. Strain the soup into a large bowl and discard everything in the strainer. Cool the soup and refrigerate overnight. Remove the fat that has hardened on the surface. (For a really superb soup, start again, using this broth, with a second batch of vegetables and a second fowl. You may need to add a bit more cold water to cover the fowl and vegetables.)

Before serving, reheat the soup and taste carefully for seasoning. It will surely need salt, and perhaps pepper. *Makes 5 to 6 quarts.*

Chicken Noodle Soup

8 cups chicken soup

1/2 pound thin noodles

Bring the soup to a boil in a saucepan and add the noodles. Lower the heat and simmer for 10 minutes, until the noodles are done. Serve with fresh snipped dill. *Makes 6 to 8 servings.*

Goose or Turkey Soup

*T*his economical idea is what every American, Jew or not, ought to make after Thanksgiving, or whenever he or she or they have splurged on goose. It's as easy as duck soup. In fact, it is duck soup if you substitute two duck carcasses for the goose or turkey called for here.

◆　　　◆　　　◆

Carcass from a cooked goose or turkey, along with wing tips, skin, trimmed drumsticks, and any other available scraps
2 large onions, quartered
2 large carrots, scraped and coarsely chopped
2 celery stalks with their leaves, coarsely chopped
1 small bunch of parsley
10 black peppercorns, crushed

Break up the carcass and place it, along with the skin, bones, and scraps, in a large soup pot. Cover with cold water and bring to a boil. Skim as foam rises to the surface. Add the onions, carrots, celery, parsley, and peppercorns. Lower the heat, partially cover the pot, and simmer for at least 2 1/2 hours.

Strain the stock through a fine sieve into a large bowl. Trim off any meat from the bones before discarding them. Press the vegetables in the sieve with the back of a wooden spoon to extract all liquid before discarding them. Let the stock cool and then refrigerate it. The fat will harden and rise to the surface; remove it with a metal spoon. Reheat the stock before serving.

Serve with mandlen (see page 53), matzo balls (see page 149), kreplach (see page 52), freshly cooked carrots, or noodles, along with any bits of meat trimmed from the bones or leftover from the main feast. *Makes 1 1/2 to 2 quarts.*

Beef Stock

*O*n a torpid Sunday in January, you will be glad for the bubbling soup pot that is working to store away stock for the many soups you will then be able to make in a trice. If you have a big enough pot and a large freezer, you can multiply the quantities here as many times as you like and have even more stock to hand. Freeze in small batches for easy defrosting.

◆　　　◆　　　◆

4 pounds soup bones
5 carrots, scraped and quartered
5 onions, peeled and quartered
4 pounds lean brisket or chuck
1 celery stalk with leaves
1 small bunch of parsley
Salt
Freshly ground black pepper

Put the bones, 2 carrots, and 2 onions in a large soup pot and cover with 3 to 4 quarts water. Bring slowly to a boil and skim any scum as it rises to the surface. When froth stops rising, partially cover and simmer for 2 to 3 hours. Let cool, then strain the stock and discard the solids. Refrigerate until cold. Remove the hardened fat.

Return the stock to the washed-out kettle and add the meat. If the stock doesn't cover the meat, add up to 2 cups cold water. Again, skim the surface until foam stops rising; adding an ice cube or two to the soup will speed the process.

Add the remaining vegetables, along with the parsley, salt, and pepper. Partially cover the pot and simmer gently until the meat is tender, about 3 hours. Remove the meat and reserve as boiled beef.

Wet a dish towel and squeeze out as much water as possible. Line a colander with the damp cloth and strain the stock into a bowl. Let cool, then refrigerate overnight. Lift off the hardened fat before using. The stock freezes well and will keep in the refrigerator for a day or two. *Makes 3 quarts.*

Schav

Some people call this sour-grass soup. The French call it *soupe à l'oseille*. By whatever name, sorrel is a leafy green that goes well with fish if prepared like spinach. This soup could be made richer by substituting chicken stock for the water, but it would lose some of its clean tartness.

◆　　◆　　◆

1 pound fresh sorrel
3 eggs plus 1 extra yolk
Lemon juice
Salt
Freshly ground black pepper

Carefully wash the sorrel leaves in several changes of cold water. Separate the leaves from the stems and hard ribs. Coarsely chop the trimmed leaves (you should have 6 to 7 cups). Tie the ribs and stems together securely in a bundle.

Put the sorrel leaves and the bundle of ribs and stems in a large nonreactive saucepan with 8 cups of water. Bring to a boil, lower the heat, and simmer for 20 to 30 minutes, until the leaves are soft and starting to disintegrate. Remove and discard the bundle of ribs and stems.

In a large bowl, beat the eggs and the extra yolk with a fork until the whites and yolks are just combined. Slowly beat in the hot soup. When 3 or 4 cups have been added, trickle the egg mixture back into the saucepan, beating constantly. Pour the soup back and forth between the pot and bowl to cool it more quickly.

Let the soup cool and refrigerate until cold. Before serving, season the soup with lemon juice, salt, and pepper to taste. Serve with sour cream. *Makes 6 to 8 servings.*

Schav is a sophisticated taste of spring from the shtetl.

KREPLACH

Kreplach is a Yiddish cognate of crêpe, the delicate French pancake. And these stuffed dumplings do start out as a thin rolled dough that may have once reminded someone of a crêpe. Better to think of them as Jewish ravioli (but if you get carried away by this notion and serve them straight from the pot with Parmesan cheese, they won't be Jewish any more, just treyf). Eat them in chicken soup or by themselves, fried in shmaltz.

◆　　　◆　　　◆

NOODLE DOUGH

*2 cups unbleached flour, plus additional for
    kneading and rolling*

2 eggs

1 tablespoon water, at room temperature

1/2 teaspoon salt

MEAT OR CHICKEN FILLING

1 tablespoon shmaltz or margarine

1/2 cup minced onions

*1/2 pound raw ground beef or 1 cup cooked,
    ground chicken*

Salt

Freshly ground black pepper

1 teaspoon chopped parsley

Make the noodle dough: Measure the flour out onto a board. Make a well in the center and put in the eggs, water, and salt. Break up the yolks with a wooden spoon and stir. Using your hands, gradually incorporate the flour into the eggs and water. Knead the dough with your hands for 10 minutes or in a standing mixer with the dough hook for 5 minutes. Add more flour if the dough is sticky, or up to 1 additional tablespoon water if it's dry and crumbly. Form the dough into a ball, wrap in plastic wrap or wax paper, and set aside unrefrigerated for 30 minutes.

Make the filling: Heat the shmaltz or margarine in a heavy skillet. Add the onions and sauté until soft but not brown. Add the ground beef, salt, and pepper. Cook until the meat is no longer pink. Remove from the heat and add the parsley. If you are using cooked chicken, add the cooked onions to it along with salt, pepper, and parsley.

On a floured board, roll out one third or half of the dough to a thickness of about 1/8 inch. Trim off any rough edges and save for rerolling. Cut the dough into 2- to 2 1/2- inch squares. Fill each square with a teaspoonful of filling. Fold the dough in half over the filling to make a triangle. Pinch the edges together to seal. If the dough doesn't stick, moisten the edges with wet fingers and seal. Pull two corners together and pinch them so they stick. Repeat with the remaining dough and filling. Let the kreplach stand on a floured board for 15 or 20 minutes before cooking them in a large quantity of boiling salted water for 20 to 25 minutes. Drain the kreplach and add to chicken soup or fry them in shmaltz or margarine to serve as an appetizer or side dish. *Makes 24 to 30 kreplach.*

SOUP MANDLEN

*M*andlen means almonds, and that is what these little soup crackers must have suggested to Jewish cooks long ago.

◆   ◆   ◆

3 eggs
3 tablespoons vegetable oil
1 teaspoon salt
1 1/2 to 2 cups unbleached flour

Preheat the oven to 375 degrees. Lightly grease a cookie sheet or jellyroll pan.

Combine the eggs with 1 1/2 tablespoons of the oil. Add the salt and 1 1/2 cups of the flour. Add more flour, if necessary, to make a soft but not sticky dough.

Divide the dough into 8 or 10 pieces— small enough to make rolling between the palms of your hands easy. Roll each piece of dough into a 1/2-inch-thick rope; cut each rope into 1/2-inch pieces and place on the prepared pan.

Bake for 20 to 30 minutes, shaking the pan occasionally so the mandlen color evenly. They are done when nicely browned and firm to the touch. Let cool to room temperature before storing in an airtight container. *Makes about 5 dozen.*

3

Fish

◆ ◆ ◆

All the recipes in this chapter center around pickled, cured, or canned fish. This does not imply that Jews didn't or don't eat fresh fish. My paternal grandfather, an immigrant from the Russian city now called Dnepropetrovsk, operated a fish market in Detroit where fresh lake trout and whitefish were usually for sale. In the old country, he had encountered similar fish, in particular the zander or pike perch. But this very sameness, which makes fish from all over the world hard to distinguish except with rough characterizations such as "firm, white, fleshy" as opposed to "oily, dark," is what has prevented a specifically Jewish aura from hovering around fresh fish dishes. A bass is a bass is a bass. But a herring, pickled or salted, carries with it in this country a whiff of another time and place. Clearly, millions of non-Jews in northern Europe ate and eat cured herring; however, in this country, the largest group to continue to do so is Jewish. In any case, herring, particularly herring prepared in certain now canonical ways, is considered to be Jewish food.

For the modern diet from the ancienne cuisine, fried herring balls (page 56), potato salad (page 134), and health salad (page 135).

HERRING WITH POTATOES

Without a doubt, the addition of chicken fat to herring marks a dish as Jewish. Here the combination also includes potato and apple, and is baked.

◆   ◆   ◆

1 1/2 pounds all-purpose potatoes
6 pickled or salted herrings (about 1 1/2 pounds)
1 cup chopped onions
2 1/2 tablespoons shmaltz
1/4 cup bread crumbs (either unseasoned commercial or homemade from stale white bread)
1 tart apple, peeled, cored, and grated

Preheat the oven to 375 degrees

Boil the potatoes until tender. Drain, peel, and slice.

Rinse and dice the herring, removing any bones.

Sauté the onions in 1 tablespoon shmaltz until soft but not browned.

Brush an 8-inch gratin dish or other ovenproof casserole with some of the remaining shmaltz. Sprinkle with half the bread crumbs. Spread a layer of potatoes over the bread crumbs. Cover with a layer of herring, then onions, and then apple. Continue layering in this order, ending with a layer of potatoes. Sprinkle with the remaining bread crumbs and dot with the remaining shmaltz. Bake in the preheated oven for 35 to 45 minutes, until the top is lightly browned. *Makes 4 to 6 servings.*

FRIED HERRING BALLS

These are really shmaltz herring croquettes. A little trouble, but easier than going back to Minsk to tap into your roots.

◆   ◆   ◆

1 cup minced onions
2 tablespoons shmaltz or vegetable oil
1 cup bread crumbs (either unseasoned commercial or homemade from stale white bread)
2 eggs
1/2 pound pickled herring fillets, minced almost to a paste
2 teaspoons lemon juice
Freshly ground black pepper
Vegetable oil for frying

Cook the onions slowly in the shmaltz or vegetable oil until translucent. Add 1/2 cup bread crumbs and cook for a minute or two. Cool.

Beat the eggs just to combine. Add the cooled onion–bread crumb mixture. Stir in the minced herring and the lemon juice.

Moisten your hands and roll the mixture into walnut-size balls. Roll the balls in the remaining bread crumbs, seasoned with pepper. Refrigerate for at least 30 minutes or up to 2 hours.

Heat the oil in a heavy skillet and fry the herring balls until brown on all sides. Drain for a minute on paper towels and serve with lemon wedges. *Makes 16 to 18 herring balls.*

SALMON LOAF OR RING

*D*o not turn up your nose at the idea of canned salmon. Tradition is tradition. You could, of course, prepare a salmon loaf with fresh salmon, and it would probably be a fine thing. You could even call it a *terrine de saumon*. Why not? Because it would have nothing to do with this well-known and beloved haimish dish, which really does depend for its texture and flavor on starting with canned fish. Myself, I happen to like canned salmon—not as a substitute for fresh but as a separate preparation of a versatile fish.

◆　　　◆　　　◆

1 can (15 1/2-ounce) salmon
1 cup chopped onions
1/4 pound mushrooms, diced (about 1 1/2 cups)
2 tablespoons butter or margarine
1/2 cup bread crumbs (either unseasoned commercial or homemade from stale white bread)
1 cup milk
2 tablespoons lemon juice
3 eggs, lightly beaten
Freshly ground black pepper

Preheat the oven to 350 degrees. Lightly grease a 9 x 5-inch loaf pan or a 6-cup ring mold.

Drain the salmon and pick over carefully, discarding any bones and skin. Flake the salmon into a mixing bowl.

Slowly cook the onions and mushrooms in the butter or margarine until most of the liquid given off by the mushrooms has evaporated. Add to the salmon along with the remaining ingredients and mix well; the mixture will be quite loose but the liquid will be absorbed during cooking.

Spoon the mixture into the prepared loaf pan or ring mold and bake for 1 hour, until the liquid is absorbed and the loaf is beginning to brown around the edges. Unmold. Serve hot or warm, in slices. *Makes 6 servings.*

LOX AND ONIONS AND EGGS

*L*ox is, from a certain point of view, merely a phonetic spelling of the standard German word for salmon, *Lachs*. But we know better. Lox is a lusty, salt-cured form of salmon that Jews eat on Sunday mornings with cream cheese and bagels. Uptown Jews sometimes substitute unsalted smoked salmon, usually referred to as Novy (a Slavicization of Nova Scotia, where most of the smoked salmon sold in New York delis was once produced). To me, this is one of the more foolish forms of assimilation eating away at Jewish solidarity in the Diaspora. Ultra-refined, lightly smoked salmon should be reserved for ultra-refined banqueting. At brunch, I want to *taste* the fish I've sandwiched between two bagel halves with a lot of cream cheese. I'm also looking for the same bold flavor in this classic Jewish contribution to the literature of scrambled eggs. Frankly, I think that if you are going to insist on chopping up fancy Novy for this dish, you should forget the onions, so that nothing interferes with your fantasy of breakfasting in first class on the QE2.

◆　　　◆　　　◆

1 tablespoon butter or margarine
1/3 cup minced onions
2 ounces lox or smoked salmon, chopped
2 eggs, beaten just to combine whites and yolks

Melt the butter or margarine in a small skillet and cook the onions over low heat for a few minutes, until very soft but not brown. Add the lox and cook for just a moment or two. Add the eggs, turn the heat to very low, and gently stir, combining the eggs, lox, and onions. Keep stirring until the eggs are set. Serve immediately. *Makes 1 serving.*

Poultry

◆ ◆ ◆

Chicken fricassee with meatballs (page 61),
from start to finish.

ROAST CHICKEN

Why is this a Jewish roast chicken? I'll tell you why. The main reason is not the relatively trivial matter of the margarine substituting for butter in a meat dish. The real reason is that a hundred million Sabbaths have begun on Friday nights throughout the Jewish universe with a roast chicken—often, I'm sorry to say, not so juicy a roast chicken as this one will be if you follow the directions and don't get distracted by other anxieties. A roast chicken encourages getting distracted by other anxieties, because it just sits there in the oven like a lox, roasting. That, of course, is why Jewish housewives, a.k.a. queens of the Sabbath and women of valor, have roasted chickens on the eve of the day of rest. They needed a dish that could be "put up" and left to cook on its own after the crack of sundown left them unable to continue the normal work of the kitchen. Furthermore, in the far-off world of the shtetl, a chicken was a festive fowl, not some mass-produced and cheap-jack bird churned out in a factory, but the top of the pecking order of banquet foods.

◆   ◆   ◆

One 4- to 5-pound chicken
Salt
Freshly ground black pepper
2 cups chopped onions
2 carrots, scraped and sliced into 1-inch chunks
4 tablespoons cold margarine, cut into bits
3 pounds small new potatoes, uniform in size,
*   parboiled and peeled if necessary (optional)*
1 cup chicken soup (see page 48)

Preheat the oven to 400 degrees.

Wash and dry the chicken. Rub salt and pepper into the skin as well as inside the chicken. Place a small handful of the onions inside the chicken.

Strew the carrots and remaining onions in a roasting pan. Scatter the margarine over the vegetables. Place a rack over the vegetables and sit the chicken, breast side down, on the rack. Put the potatoes, if you are using them, around the chicken. Place the pan in the oven and immediately turn the heat down to 350 degrees. Baste the chicken from time to time with the pan juices and add a little water to the pan if the vegetables start to burn. After the chicken has been roasting for about an hour, turn it breast side up for the final 25 or 30 minutes of cooking. When the juices run clear when a thigh is pierced and the legs move easily in their sockets, the chicken is done; calculate 20 to 25 minutes per pound.

Remove the chicken to a carving board. Let it rest for 5 minutes, then carve. Put the potatoes and some of the browned onions into a heatproof serving dish and keep warm in the oven. Place the roasting pan over two burners and add the strained chicken stock. Bring to a boil and scrape up the brown bits clinging to the pan. Boil for a few minutes. Skim off the surface fat and pass with the chicken. *Makes 3 to 6 servings.*

Chicken Fricassee with Meatballs

*T*his dish was traditionally made with leftover bits of the chicken: beaks, necks, feet, and perhaps one leg or wing. Nowadays, the beaks and the feet are harder to get than the breast so this recipe calls for a whole chicken, cut up. Tomatoes are another North American addition. If you want to be totally authentic, eliminate the tomatoes in the recipe and stir in 1 teaspoon paprika before you add the chicken pieces and 1 to 1 1/2 cups water after you've added the chicken. The fricassee is delicious both ways.

◆ ◆ ◆

3 to 4 cups chopped onions
4 tablespoons vegetable oil or margarine
1 teaspoon tomato paste
2 cups chopped canned tomatoes with 1 cup of liquid from the can (most of the contents of a 35-ounce can)
One 3-pound chicken (including all giblets, but not the liver), cut into 8 to 10 pieces
Salt
Finely ground black pepper

MEATBALLS
1 pound ground beef
1 egg
2 teaspoons minced garlic
2 tablespoons matzo meal or bread crumbs
Salt
Freshly ground black pepper

In a large deep skillet that has a tight-fitting lid, cook the onions in the oil or margarine until soft and lightly colored, 15 to 20 minutes.

Stir in the tomato paste and the chopped tomatoes and their liquid. Add the chicken pieces and the giblets. The liquid should come about halfway up the chicken but the pieces should not be submerged. Cover the skillet and simmer the chicken for 20 minutes. Add salt and pepper to taste.

Meanwhile, make the meatballs by combining all the ingredients in a large bowl. Form the mixture into balls about 1 inch in diameter (about 1 scant tablespoon). Carefully add the meatballs to the skillet, moving the chicken pieces around to make room.

Re-cover the skillet and cook for an additional 20 minutes. You can serve the fricassee immediately, but it also takes well to reheating. If you have the time, remove the chicken and meatballs, strain the broth, and remove the fat. Serve with rice or noodles.
Makes 4 to 6 servings.

OVERLEAF: *Chicken in the pot (page 64).*

CHICKEN IN THE POT

Chicken in the pot may sound a bit infra dig, but really no more so than the honored French dish *poule au pot*, which is an exact translation of chicken in the pot and which has no kneidlach in it. Kneidlach are serious dumplings, made with matzo meal and best known as part of the Passover menu. Chicken in the pot is a serious main dish, especially when made with a serious chicken soup.

◆　　　◆　　　◆

One 3-pound chicken
3 large carrots, scraped and cut into thin strips
　about 1 inch long
2 celery stalks, cut into thin strips about 1 inch
　long
1 large turnip, peeled and cut in the same shape
　as the carrots and celery
3 parsnips, scraped and cut into thick strips
　about 1 inch long
2 cups coarsely chopped leeks, including some
　green
8 cups chicken soup (see page 48)
Kneidlach (see page 149)
1/2 pound thin egg noodles, cooked

Put the chicken and all the vegetables in a pot just large enough for them and the chicken soup—too large a pot and the chicken will not be covered with liquid. Add the chicken soup and bring to a boil. Lower the heat, partially cover the pot, and cook at a gentle simmer for 1 hour. Skim from time to time.

While the chicken is cooking, make the kneidlach and cook the noodles.

To serve, remove the chicken and carve it into 8 to 10 pieces. Put some soup and vegetables, a kneidlach or two, some noodles, and a piece of chicken in each of 8 warmed soup bowls. *Makes 8 servings.*

CHICKEN AND DUMPLINGS

*T*his is a streamlined version of chicken in the pot, made with a chicken cut in pieces instead of a whole chicken, diced vegetables, and smaller non-matzo dumplings.

◆   ◆   ◆

One 3 1/2- to 4-pound chicken, cut into
  8 pieces
2 tablespoons vegetable oil
1 cup chopped onions
1 cup chopped carrots
1/2 cup diced celery
1 tablespoon paprika
Salt
Freshly ground black pepper
About 2 cups chicken soup (see page 48) or
  water

DUMPLINGS
1 egg
2 tablespoons shmaltz, melted
1 teaspoon salt
1 1/2 cups flour

Brown the chicken pieces quickly in the oil in a large wide casserole. Add the onions, carrots, celery, paprika, and salt and pepper. Stir for a moment or two, pushing the chicken aside to brown the vegetables lightly. Add enough chicken soup or water to come about halfway up the chicken pieces. Cover the pot and cook at a gentle simmer for about 1 hour.

Lightly beat the egg with the shmaltz and 1/4 cup water. Slowly mix in the salt and flour. Mix vigorously with a wooden spoon for a few minutes, until the dough is well combined and comes away from the sides of the bowl. Set aside for 30 minutes.

Bring a large quantity of salted water to a boil. Break off bits of the dough with a tablespoon dipped in the boiling water. Moisten your fingers in cold water and neaten the dough into small ovals. Drop the dumplings into the water; if they stick to the spoon, immerse the spoon in the water—the dumplings will fall into the pot. Cook until the dumplings rise to the surface. Remove with a slotted spoon and drain. Serve immediately with the chicken. *Makes 6 servings.*

OVERLEAF: *Roast goose (page 68) is the big bird of the Old World, an ample feast here amply stuffed with potato and garnished with honeyed carrots (page 114).*

Roast Goose with Potato Stuffing

*I*t was a bright night in the shtetl when a family sat down to eat this goose. If you have trouble imagining the scene, think of the unconfined joy in the Cratchit household when Scrooge brings them a goose for Christmas, and multiply by 17. Tiny Tim's mom did not make potato stuffing or helzel (see following recipe), but the stuffing suggested here rises to the occasion, with grated potato, goose gribenes and innards, and matzo meal.

A goose is still special in Eastern Europe. I priced one recently at sixty dollars in the Moscow Central Market. They are not that much cheaper in the Free-World Diaspora.

◆   ◆   ◆

One 7- to 8-pound goose, liver and gizzard
  reserved
1 cup chopped onions
2 to 3 cups grated and drained peeled potatoes
  (about 1 1/2 pounds)
1 egg, lightly beaten
1 tablespoon matzo meal
Salt
Freshly ground black pepper

Preheat the oven to 450 degrees.

Remove as much fat as possible from the goose and render it as for shmaltz (see page 28). Reserve the gribenes and fat separately.

Heat 1/4 cup of the goose fat in a skillet, add the onions, and cook slowly for about 10 minutes. Meanwhile, grind or chop the goose liver and peeled gizzard. Add to the onions along with the potatoes and cook for 4 or 5 minutes, stirring constantly. Cool for 5 minutes, then add the egg, matzo meal, reserved gribenes, and salt and pepper.

Rub the outside of the goose with salt and pepper. Stuff the goose with the potato mixture. Sew the openings closed with a trussing needle or fasten with metal skewers.

Place the goose on a rack in a roasting pan, breast side down. Pierce around the legs with a fork. Pour 1 cup boiling water into the roasting pan and place in the oven. After 10 minutes, turn the heat down to 325 degrees. Roast the goose for 2 hours, basting with the pan juices from time to time and pricking around the legs with a fork. Turn the goose breast side up and cook for an additional 30 minutes to 1 hour, basting the breast with some of the reserved rendered goose fat. Remove from the oven when the goose tests done: the legs should move easily in their sockets.

Remove the goose to a board. Spoon the stuffing into a serving bowl and carve the goose as you would a chicken. *Makes 6 servings.*

HELZEL
STUFFED GOOSE NECK

I know. It sounds weird and excessively
ethnic. But the real problem with this
incredibly delicious "natural" sausage is
finding an intact goose neck. This is
where live poultry markets come in. Most
cities have them, and they can be
persuaded to save the neck and keep the
all-important skin intact. Helzel is worth
whatever trouble it takes.

◆   ◆   ◆

Skin of 1 goose neck
1/4 cup grated onions
1/2 cup rendered goose fat or shmaltz
1 1/2 cups flour
Salt
Freshly ground black pepper
Paprika

Sew up one end of the goose neck. Mix
together all the remaining ingredients and
stuff into the goose neck skin. Sew up the
other end. Roast in the same pan with the
goose (see opposite).

Meat

♦ ♦ ♦

Lamb stew (page 85) with mamaliga (page 98),
the maize-gold Romanian version of polenta, cornmeal's zenith.

BOILED FLANKEN

*F*lanken is the name Jews give to a cut of chuck with the ribs left in. Think of this dish as Jewish boiled beef dinner.

◆   ◆   ◆

4 pounds lean, meaty flanken
2 tablespoons vegetable oil
2 cups chopped onions
1 cup chopped carrots
1/2 cup chopped celery, along with a few celery leaves
4 parsley sprigs
Salt
6 whole black peppercorns
4 cups beef stock (see page 49) or water or a combination of the two

In a large heavy pot just large enough to hold all the ingredients, brown the flanken in the vegetable oil. Drain off the fat. Add the onions, carrots, celery, parsley, salt, and peppercorns. Pour in the stock or water and bring to a boil. Cover the pot and simmer very gently for 2 hours, or until the flanken is very tender and coming away from the bones. Strain the broth and discard the vegetables. Serve the flanken moistened with some of the broth. *Makes 4 to 6 servings.*

TSIMMES WITH MEAT

*S*ome people refer to this pot roast as flanken with dried fruit. The combination is seductive by any name. This is definitely a big tsimmes and can, of course, be prepared ahead, so as to serve a crowd conveniently.

◆   ◆   ◆

Vegetable oil
6 pounds lean, meaty flanken
Salt
Freshly ground black pepper
4 cups chopped onions
4 cups boiling water
1 pound pitted prunes
11 ounces dried apricots
2 1/2 pounds carrots, scraped and sliced
2 pounds sweet potatoes, peeled and sliced
Grated peel and juice from 1 lemon
1/2 teaspoon ground cloves
2 teaspoons grated fresh ginger
1/2 teaspoon cinnamon
Nutmeg

Film the bottom of a large heavy pot with vegetable oil over medium heat. Season the meat with salt and pepper and brown in the heated oil in batches, to avoid crowding the pot and steaming the meat. Add the onions and cook until soft. Return all meat to the pot, cover, and cook for 1 hour over very gentle heat.

Meanwhile, pour the boiling water over the prunes and apricots and let soak for 30 minutes.

Preheat the oven the 325 degrees.

After the meat has cooked on the stove for an hour, add the prunes and apricots and their soaking liquid to the pot, along with the carrots, sweet potatoes, lemon peel and juice, cloves, ginger, cinnamon, and a few gratings of nutmeg. Replace the cover and bake the tsimmes for 2 1/2 to 3 hours. Remove the cover for the last 30 to 45 minutes; the top of the tsimmes should brown lightly. *Makes 8 to 10 servings.*

Pot Roast of Brisket

Another cook-ahead special for winter entertaining.

◆　　　◆　　　◆

2 cloves garlic, mashed through a press
Salt
Freshly ground black pepper
5 pounds first-cut brisket
2 large onions, peeled and cut into eighths
2 pounds carrots, scraped
1 cup dry red wine

Preheat the oven to 500 degrees.

Make a paste with the garlic and salt and pepper; rub the paste into both sides of the brisket. Put the meat in a roasting pan, fat side up, and roast until the meat is very brown, 15 to 20 minutes.

Lower the heat to 350 degrees. Remove the brisket and strew the onions over the bottom of the pan. Replace the meat and put the carrots on top. Pour the wine into the pan.

Cover the meat with aluminum foil and roast for 2 to 2 1/2 hours, until the meat is tender. Remove the meat and carrots to a plate and pour the liquid and onions into a bowl. Refrigerate or freeze briefly until the fat rises to the surface and can easily be removed. Put the liquid and onions in a processor or blender and purée. Slice the meat and put it back in the roasting pan for a few minutes to heat with the gravy. Serve with the carrots. *Makes 8 to 10 servings.*

Braised Short Ribs

6 pounds short ribs, cut into 2- to 3-inch pieces
Flour, for dredging
Salt
Freshly ground black pepper
5 tablespoons vegetable oil
4 cups chopped onions
1 tablespoon chopped garlic
2 teaspoons dried thyme
1 1/2 cups beef stock (see page 49)

Lightly dredge the ribs in flour seasoned with salt and pepper.

Heat 3 tablespoons vegetable oil in a heavy skillet. Add the ribs and brown on all sides in batches; do not crowd the skillet or the ribs will steam rather than brown. Drain the ribs on paper towels.

In a pan that is large enough to hold the ribs comfortably and has a tight-fitting cover, heat the remaining vegetable oil. Add the onions and garlic and cook very slowly until the onions are soft and wilted but not brown, about 15 to 20 minutes.

Place the browned ribs over the onions and add the thyme and beef stock. Bring to a boil, cover, and simmer on top of the stove or in a preheated 300-degree oven for about 1 hour, until the meat is tender when pierced with a fork. It may take longer, depending on the quality of the meat.

If you have the time, strain and refrigerate the juices. The fat will harden and rise to the top and can easily be removed. Reheat the dish for 15 or 20 minutes before serving. If you don't have the time to refrigerate the juices, skim off as much fat as you can before serving. *Makes 6 or 7 servings.*

Potted Meatballs with Potatoes

Meatballs may have originated in the Middle East. In Morocco, cumin is often added to them; the paprika is an Ashkenazic ingredient.

◆　　　◆　　　◆

2 1/2 pounds ground chuck
2 eggs, lightly beaten
2 tablespoons bread crumbs or matzo meal
3 cups minced onions
3 tablespoons minced garlic
2 teaspoons ground cumin
1 tablespoon paprika
Salt
Freshly ground black pepper
3 tablespoons vegetable oil
6 carrots, scraped and cut in 1/4-inch rounds
6 medium potatoes, peeled and quartered

Combine the ground meat with the eggs, bread crumbs or matzo meal, 3/4 cup of the onions, 1 tablespoon garlic, 1 teaspoon cumin, 1 1/2 teaspoons paprika, and salt and pepper. Mix with your hands to combine thoroughly. Form meatballs about 5 to 6 inches in circumference (or smaller if you like).

Heat the oil in a large heavy skillet with a tight-fitting cover. Add the remaining onions and garlic and sauté for a few minutes, until softened. Add the remaining cumin, paprika, and the carrots. Remove the vegetables from the skillet.

Add the meatballs to the skillet and cook over medium heat, rolling them around with wooden spoon so they brown evenly. Cook only a few at a time; if you crowd the pan, the meatballs won't brown.

Put the vegetables and all the meatballs back in the skillet. Add the potatoes and 1/2 cup water. Bring to a gentle simmer, cover the pan, and cook over low heat for 45 minutes, until the potatoes are soft. *Makes 4 to 6 servings.*

Klops

Two kinds of ground meat and hard-boiled eggs make this an unusual and elegant meatloaf.

◆　　　◆　　　◆

3/4 pound ground chuck
3/4 pound ground veal
1 medium potato, peeled and grated (about 1/3 cup)
1 cup grated onions
2 raw eggs
4 cloves garlic, mashed through a press or minced
Salt
Freshly ground black pepper
2 hard-boiled eggs

Preheat the oven to 375 degrees.

With your hands, combine all the ingredients except the hard-boiled eggs. Mix well. Using half of the meat, form a round or rectangular loaf in a small pan. Lay the hard-boiled eggs, top to bottom, down the center of the loaf. Cover completely with the remaining meat and bake for about 1 hour and 15 minutes. Remove from the pan and serve hot, or let cool, refrigerate, and serve cold. *Serves 4 to 6.*

Klops is the name for this hypermeatball, stuffed with hard-boiled egg for a beautiful effect when sliced. In midwinter, a season that in Lithuania includes all months except July and early August, hot beets (page 107) and sauteed cabbage with noodles (page 96) nicely round out a meal centered on klops.

STUFFED PEPPERS

6 tablespoons raw rice
1 pound ground beef
1 medium onion, peeled
1 tablespoon minced garlic
1 egg, lightly beaten
Salt
Freshly ground black pepper
6 green bell peppers
Juice of 1/2 lemon

Partially cook the rice in a large quantity of boiling water for 5 or 6 minutes; drain.

Preheat the oven to 350 degrees.

Put the meat in a mixing bowl and grate in the onion. Add the rice, garlic, egg, and salt and pepper and mix well.

Slice off the stem end of the peppers. Remove the cores and the white ribs inside, being careful not to pierce the flesh (a grapefruit knife is useful for this). Run the peppers under cold water to remove the seeds.

Stuff the peppers with the meat mixture; don't pack it too tightly or the peppers might split.

Place the peppers in a baking dish just large enough to hold them upright, leaning against each other. Pour in enough water to come about one third of the way up the sides of the peppers. Add the lemon juice. Bake for 30 to 40 minutes, until the peppers are tender. *Makes 6 servings.*

Stuffed Cabbage

3 tablespoons margarine

1 1/2 cups coarsely chopped onions

1/2 cup packed brown sugar

One 35-ounce can peeled tomatoes packed in
    tomato juice

2 cups tomato sauce

One 3-pound green cabbage

1 small onion, peeled

2 pounds ground beef

2 eggs, lightly beaten

1/4 cup raw rice

2 tablespoons ketchup

Salt

Freshly ground black pepper

1/2 pound pitted prunes (about 1 1/2 cups)

1/2 cup raisins

Juice of 1 lemon

Melt the margarine in a large pot. Add the onions and sauté over medium heat for about 10 minutes, until they are soft and lightly colored. Add the brown sugar and stir with a wooden spoon, mashing out any lumps against the pot. Break up the tomatoes with your fingers and add them to the pot along with their juice and the tomato sauce. Cover the pot and simmer gently for about 1 hour.

While the sauce is cooking, prepare the cabbage and the filling. Cut the core out of the cabbage and discard. Place the cabbage in a large pot and cover with boiling water. Put the lid on the pot and let sit for about 15 minutes.

To prepare the filling, grate the onion directly into the meat in a bowl. Add the eggs, rice, ketchup, and salt and pepper. Mix gently with your hands. If the mixture seems too dense and heavy, mix in up to 1/2 cup warm water.

Remove the cabbage from the hot water. Peel off the leaves, one by one, without tearing them. If any leaves still seem stiff, put them back in the pot and bring the water to a boil. Remove the leaves after 2 or 3 minutes; they must be limp enough to fold without tearing. With a small sharp knife, shave off the hard ribs. The center leaves of cabbage are too small to stuff; shred these leaves and add them to the tomato sauce. The outermost leaves are too large to stuff; cut them in half.

Place about 1/3 cup of the meat mixture into the center of each cabbage leaf. Fold the leaves so as to completely enclose the filling. One by one, place the stuffed cabbage leaves in the tomato sauce. Form any leftover meat into meatballs and add them to the pot. Finally, add the prunes, raisins, and lemon juice. Cook over low heat, covered, for about 1 1/2 hours. *Makes 16 to 20 stuffed cabbage leaves, serving 6 as an entrée.*

Note: The cooked stuffed cabbage will keep in the refrigerator for several days and frozen for several months. Defrost before reheating.

Overleaf: *Cabbage stuffed with ground meat is a universal of cooking in Mittel-Europa. Bertha Grossman's has not only tomato sauce, but prunes and raisins.*

STUFFED BREAST OF VEAL

*T*his is the most economical large cut of veal you can buy, and it lends itself to stuffing. The butcher cuts a pocket in the meat; you put in what appeals to you. Almost every European cuisine has its own preferred stuffings for veal breast. Three traditional Jewish stuffing recipes follow; each makes enough to stuff a half breast. This is the time to be grateful that calves have their breasts in front and not in their hindquarters, since (as I suppose you haven't reflected before) if they didn't, veal breast would be treyf and Jewish cooks would not have dreamed up these fine stuffings for this splendid cut of meat.

◆　　　◆　　　◆

1/2 breast of veal (about 7 pounds)
1 tablespoon shmaltz or margarine
2 onions, peeled and quartered
6 carrots, scraped and chopped
2 cloves garlic, peeled and halved
Salt
Freshly ground black pepper
1 teaspoon paprika

Ask the butcher to cut as large a pocket as possible in the veal without cutting through the top or the sides.

Preheat the oven to 375 degrees.

Place the shmaltz in a roasting pan and scatter the onions, carrots, and garlic over the bottom of the pan.

Wash and dry the breast. Rub the inside with salt and pepper. Stuff the pocket with the stuffing and close with metal skewers. Set the breast on the vegetables in the roasting pan and rub the outside with salt, pepper, and the paprika.

Place in the oven for 30 minutes. Add 1 cup water to the pan and lower the heat to 350 degrees. Cook for another 30 minutes, then cover the pan with aluminum foil or the pan's own cover. Cook for another 2 1/2 to 3 hours, until the meat is very tender when pierced with a fork.

Remove the meat to a carving board and strain the juices into a saucepan. Press the solids to extract all juices. Skim as much fat as you can and heat the gravy. Slice the veal between the bones and serve with the gravy. *Makes 4 to 6 servings.*

Matzo Ball Stuffing

This recipe uses the same ingredients as matzo balls (with the addition of onions and parsley). It should be made just before stuffing the veal.

3/4 cup minced onions
3 tablespoons shmaltz
4 eggs
1 cup matzo meal
Salt
Freshly ground black pepper
2 tablespoons minced parsley

Cook the onions in 1 tablespoon shmaltz for 10 minutes or so, until very soft but not colored.

Beat the eggs with 1/3 cup water. Add the remaining 2 tablespoons shmaltz, the matzo meal, and salt and pepper. Add the onions and parsley. Mix well.

Potato Stuffing

This is the same mixture that is used for Latkes. Use half the quantities specified in the master recipe (see page 100) and add 1 tablespoon minced parsley. Make the stuffing just before you are ready to stuff the veal.

Liver and Bread Stuffing

This is an adaptation of a recipe collected by Edouard de Pomiane for *The Jews of Poland* (1929).

6 slices day-old white bread, soaked in water
*   and squeezed dry*
1 pound calf's liver
4 medium onions, peeled and finely chopped
Salt
Freshly ground black pepper
3 tablespoons shmaltz
2 egg yolks

Chop the bread together with the calf's liver. Mix in half the chopped onions and salt and pepper.

Heat the shmaltz and cook the rest of the onions along with the liver mixture. Let the mixture cool, then blend in the egg yolks.

Stuffed breast of veal (page 80), ready to serve.

Veal Stew

3 tablespoons margarine or shmaltz

2 cups chopped onions

1 tablespoon paprika

3 pounds boneless shoulder of veal, cubed

Salt

Freshly ground black pepper

1 teaspoon caraway seeds

1 cup diced green bell pepper

1 tablespoon minced garlic

1 tablespoon white vinegar

1/2 teaspoon tomato paste dissolved in 1 cup
   warm water

Melt the margarine or shmaltz in a large heavy skillet. Add the onions and paprika and cook slowly until very soft, about 10 minutes. Add the remaining ingredients and bring to a boil. Lower the heat, cover the skillet, and cook very gently for about 2 hours, until the veal is tender. *Makes 5 to 6 servings.*

Braised Shoulder of Veal

One 2 1/2- to 3-pound boneless shoulder of
   veal, rolled and tied

2 tablespoons vegetable oil or margarine

1/2 cup chopped carrots

1 cup chopped onions

2 teaspoons minced garlic

1 tablespoon paprika

Salt

Freshly ground black pepper

Dry the veal with paper towels. Brown the meat on all sides in a heavy casserole in the oil or margarine. Remove the meat.

Add the carrots, onions, garlic, paprika, and salt and pepper to the casserole. Sauté for a few minutes, until the onion softens. Replace the meat. Add water to a depth of 1 inch. Cover the pot and simmer very gently for 2 to 2 1/2 hours, until the meat is very tender. Check to make sure there is always water in the pan.

Place the veal on a cutting board, remove the strings, and let rest for 10 minutes. Thinly slice the veal and serve with the pan juices. Alternatively, strain the pan juices into a saucepan and press down on the vegetables in the sieve to mash them into the sauce. Spoon the sauce over the meat and serve. *Makes 4 to 5 servings.*

Braised Lamb Shanks

Only the forequarters of ruminant animals are kosher. I don't believe there is a taste difference between front and hind legs, but if you want to hew to tradition, buy your shanks from a kosher butcher. Not only will the meat be officially kashered, but you won't have to wonder if you really can distinguish between the foreshanks and hindshanks that are all mixed together in the meat case at the supermarket.

◆　　　◆　　　◆

4 meaty lamb (fore) shanks (about
　3 1/2 pounds)
3 tablespoons vegetable oil
1 cup chopped onions
10 cloves garlic, unpeeled
Salt
Freshly ground black pepper
1 tablespoon lemon juice
1 bay leaf

Dry the lamb shanks with paper towels. Brown the shanks in the oil in a large heavy skillet in which they will fit comfortably in one layer. Then scatter the onions and garlic over them. Add salt, pepper, lemon juice, bay leaf, and 1/2 cup of water. Cover and cook over very low heat for 1 1/2 hours, until the meat is very tender. Add more water if the pan seems dry.

Remove the shanks to a serving platter. Raise the heat and scrape up any brown bits from the bottom of the pan. Skin the garlic cloves by mashing them against the side of the pan with a wooden spoon. Discard the skins and mash the garlic into the pan juices. Discard the bay leaf and pour the pan juices over the shanks. *Makes 4 servings.*

LAMB STEW

3 pounds boneless lamb shoulder, cut into
    2-inch cubes

3 tablespoons vegetable oil

2 cups chopped onions

Salt

Freshly ground black pepper

2 cups beef stock (see page 49)

1 bay leaf

2 cloves garlic, peeled and mashed through a
    press

6 carrots, scraped

1 large parsnip, scraped

4 small turnips, peeled

2 pounds potatoes, peeled

1 cup shelled fresh or frozen peas

1/2 pound fresh green beans, trimmed and cut
    into 1/2-inch pieces

Dry the lamb with paper towels. Heat the oil in a heavy casserole and brown the lamb in batches: don't crowd the pot.

Pour off most of the fat from the casserole. Add the onions and sauté for a few minutes; as you stir the onions, scrape up the brown bits on the bottom of the pot. Return the meat and toss with salt and pepper. Add enough beef stock to barely cover the meat. Add the bay leaf and garlic. Bring to a simmer. Cover the pot and cook very slowly for 1 hour.

While the meat is cooking, prepare the vegetables. Quarter the carrots and slice into 1 1/2-inch pieces. Cut the parsnip to roughly the same dimension. Halve the turnips and the potatoes and slice them. If the potatoes are large, halve the slices.

After the lamb has cooked for an hour, stir in the prepared root vegetables. Continue cooking for 15 minutes, until the vegetables are soft.

If you have time, pour the stew into a colander set over a large bowl. Wipe out the casserole and return the meat and vegetables. Refrigerate or freeze the juices until the fat hardens at the top and can easily be removed, then return the juices to the meat and reheat. If you want to serve the stew immediately, remove what fat you can with a large spoon. Add the peas and green beans and cook for 5 minutes more. Remove the bay leaf before serving. *Makes 6 servings.*

SALAMI AND EGGS

1 teaspoon oil
Three 1/2-inch-thick slices salami, cut into strips
2 eggs, beaten to combine whites and yolks

Heat the oil in a skillet and fry the salami strips until they brown lightly, tossing with a wooden spoon to color evenly. Add the eggs and cook until set, about 1 minute. Turn and brown the other side. Alternatively, you can scramble the eggs, mixing gently with a wooden spoon until they are done as you like them. *Makes 1 serving.*

Salami and eggs, survival food for Jewish bachelors and therefore rich with the nostalgia of lost freedom for Jewish husbands. Serve with care.

INNARDS

*I*t is not well known in the world at large or among emancipated Jews that innards are, or were, a major part of Jewish cooking. The meat menu commonly included sweetbreads and brains, lungs, spleen, even udder and, in the Middle East, penis. Here, then, are a few representative dishes. Tongue and kishke are still popular. Spleen and lungs have essentially vanished from American tables. In most places, many of the basic meats are unavailable even by special order.

◆   ◆   ◆

Pickled Tongue

One 5-pound pickled beef tongue
2 onions, peeled and quartered
3 cloves garlic, peeled and halved
2 bay leaves

Wash the tongue and put it in a deep casserole with the remaining ingredients and water to cover. Bring to a boil, skim, and simmer, partially covered, for 2 1/2 to 3 1/2 hours, until tender when pierced with a fork.

If you plan to serve the tongue hot, let it remain in the broth until serving. If you plan to serve the tongue cold, let it cool completely in the broth, then store it in 2 to 3 cups of the strained broth.

Remove the skin, bones, and root end of the tongue. Slice and serve with mustard or with Sweet and Sour Sauce (see below). If you are serving the tongue with the sauce, reheat it in the sauce for 5 to 8 minutes. *Makes 6 to 8 servings.*

Sweet and Sour Sauce

1 cup chopped onions
2 tablespoons vegetable oil
2 tablespoons flour
2 cups strained tongue broth (see above)
3 tablespoons lemon juice
3 tablespoons honey
1/2 cup raisins

Slowly cook the onions in the oil. Stir in the flour and cook for a minute or two. Gradually add the tongue broth and stir until it boils. Lower the heat and add the lemon juice, honey, and raisins. Simmer for 5 minutes. *Makes about 2 cups.*

Kishke
STUFFED DERMA

Kishke has a certain inverse chic. I recall a menu at a wedding in a kosher catering palace on Long Island where every dish was listed in French, including *derma farci.*

Three 8-inch lengths of beef large intestine
   prepared as sausage casing, rinsed
1 medium onion, peeled and chopped
1/4 cup shmaltz
2 tablespoons bread crumbs
3/4 cup all-purpose flour
Salt
Freshly ground black pepper

Preheat the oven to 350 degrees.

Sew up one end of each length of intestine.

Sauté the onion in the shmaltz until browned. Stir in the bread crumbs and flour and season with salt and pepper to taste. Stuff the casing lengths with the mixture. Sew up the ends. Blanch the stuffed derma in boiling salted water for 4 minutes. Drain well.

Bake the kishke in a greased, shallow ovenproof dish for about 1 1/2 hours, until browned, basting frequently with the pan grease. *Makes 4 to 6 servings.*

Gefilte Miltz
STUFFED SPLEEN

As recently as the mid-seventies, I encountered spleen in a friend's kitchen in Brooklyn. This recipe and the one that follows it, for lungs, are adapted from Pomiane's *The Jews of Poland.* Spleen did not survive the emigration to America, perhaps because it is not an appealing food. As a first-generation American housewife who had never tasted it said recently, "We were never so poor we had to eat miltz." Neither spleen nor lung is now commonly available because the U.S. Department of Agriculture does not inspect these cuts.

Kosher salt
1 beef spleen, sliced in half lengthwise
1/2 pound beef liver, chopped
1/2 cup bread crumbs
3 onions, peeled
Freshly groung black pepper
1/4 cup shmaltz
1 egg, lightly beaten
1 carrot, scraped and cut in thin rounds
1 calves' foot, cut in pieces

Shake salt over the spleen and let sit for 1 hour. Rinse and pat dry.

Mix the liver and bread crumbs together in a bowl. Chop two of the onions and add to the liver. Season with salt and pepper.

Sauté the liver mixture in 2 tablespoons of shmaltz until the onions are lightly browned. Cool to room temperature, then beat in the egg.

Spread one of the spleen halves with the liver mixture. Top with the other piece of spleen and tie the package securely with string.

In a heavy saucepan just large enough to hold the spleen package and other ingredients, heat the remaining shmaltz. Add the spleen and brown it on all sides. Slice the remaining onion and brown it in the saucepan along with the carrot slices. Add the calf's foot pieces and enough water to cover. Bring to a boil, lower the heat, cover, and simmer for 4 hours.

Remove the bones from the calves' foot pieces, discard the string, and serve. *Makes 8 servings.*

Lungen
LUNGS

I ate lungen only once, with my father, at Lieberman's Blue Room in Detroit. I do not recall finishing my portion. Perhaps I would like lungen today, but I have no occasion to find out. Lieberman's and others like it are long gone, victims of suburban flight and the national aversion to offal.

2 tablespoons shmaltz
1 onion, peeled and chopped
2 carrots, scraped and chopped
1 pound beef lung, washed, trimmed, and diced
Salt
Freshly ground black pepper

Heat the shmaltz and sauté the onion and carrots in it until softened. Add the lung. Season with salt and pepper. Add water to cover, and bring to a boil. Lower the heat, cover, and simmer for 1 1/2 hours. *Makes 3 to 4 servings.*

Noodles, Grains, and Pancakes

♦ ♦ ♦

*Blintzes (page 103) are stuffed with cheese.
Then roll the delicate pancakes neatly, fry, and serve
while hot, for special praise at special breakfasts.*

THREE NOODLE KUGELS

A kugel is a pudding. This one is a constant feature on Sabbath and holiday tables. Lokshen is Yiddish for noodles.

◆ ◆ ◆

LOKSHEN KUGEL (MEAT)

1/3 cup shmaltz
2 cups diced onions
1/2 pound medium egg noodles
3 eggs
Gribenes (see page 28) (optional)
Salt
Freshly ground black pepper

Preheat the oven to 375 degrees. Use 1 tablespoon shmaltz to lightly grease an 8-cup ovenproof dish.

Cook the onions slowly in the remaining shmaltz until they are very soft, about 15 minutes. Raise the heat for a minute or two to brown the onions very lightly.

Meanwhile, cook the noodles in a large quantity of boiling salted water for 7 to 10 minutes, until tender; drain.

Beat the eggs lightly in a large mixing bowl. Add the noodles and the onions and the fat in which they cooked. Add the gribenes, if you have any, and salt and pepper. Turn the mixture into the prepared pan and bake for 30 to 40 minutes, until lightly browned on top. *Makes 8 servings.*

Lokshen Kugel i (dairy)

6 tablespoons butter, melted
1 pound broad egg noodles
2 cups (1 pound) cottage cheese
2 cups sour cream
4 eggs, lightly beaten
1/2 cup sugar
1/2 cup raisins
1 cup peeled and minced tart apple
1 cup plain bread crumbs
1 teaspoon cinnamon
1 teaspoon brown sugar

Preheat the oven to 350 degrees. Use some of the butter to grease a 3-quart overproof dish.

Cook the noodles in a large quantity of boiling salted water for 8 to 10 minutes, until tender; drain well.

In a large bowl, combine the cottage cheese, sour cream, eggs, sugar, raisins, and apple. Mix well. Add the drained noodles and mix again. Turn the mixture into the prepared baking dish.

Combine the bread crumbs with all but 1 tablespoon of the remaining melted butter, the cinnamon, and the brown sugar. Cover the top of the pudding with this mixture and drizzle over the remaining tablespoon of butter. Bake the kugel for 45 minutes to 1 hour, until the top is nicely browned and the kugel is bubbling. *Makes 10 to 12 servings.*

Lokshen Kugel ii (dairy)

8 tablespoons (1 stick) butter, melted
1/2 pound thin egg noodles
3 eggs
1/2 pound farmer cheese
3 1/2 ounces cream cheese
1/2 cup sugar
1 teaspoon vanilla extract
Salt
3/4 cup sour cream
1/2 cup milk
1 teaspoon cinnamon
Grated peel and juice from 1 lemon

Preheat the oven to 350 degrees. With some of the melted butter, grease a 2-quart oven-proof dish.

In a large quantity of boiling salted water, cook the noodles for 3 to 4 minutes, until tender. Drain.

Lightly beat the eggs in a large mixing bowl. Add the remaining ingredients and mix to combine well. Add the noodles and turn the mixture into the prepared pan. Bake for 35 to 45 minutes, until the top is lightly brown and the kugel is barely moist within. *Makes 8 to 10 servings.*

Overleaf: *Lokshen kugel I, noodle pudding with cheese. Plain looking but plain delicious, and really quite a complicated notion if you think about it.*

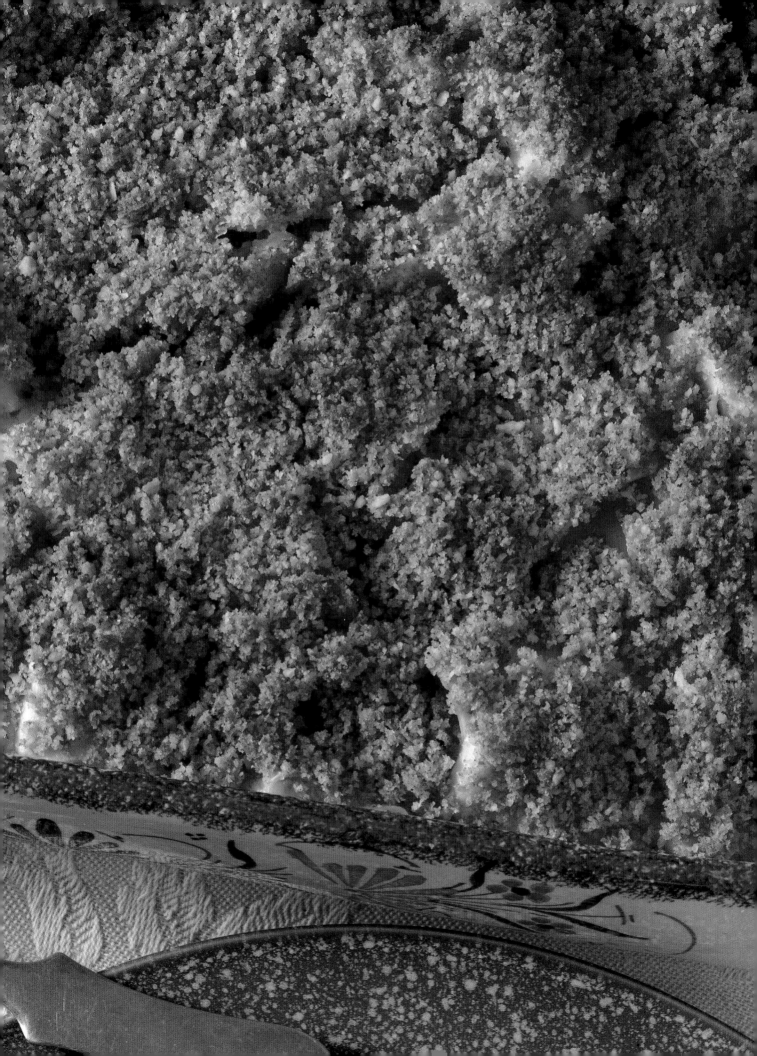

Sauteed Cabbage with Noodles

The cabbage shreds and the noodles make an interesting combination. Caraway seeds and shmaltz add two characteristic tastes of this cuisine.

◆   ◆   ◆

One 2-pound green cabbage
2 tablespoons kosher salt
4 to 8 tablespoons shmaltz or margarine
1/4 pound bowtie noodles
1/4 teaspoon caraway seeds
Salt
Freshly ground black pepper
Sugar

Remove the tough outer leaves of the cabbage, then halve and core it. Shred the cabbage and place it in a colander with the salt. Mix with your hands and let drain for 30 minutes.

Heat 4 tablespoons shmaltz or margarine in a large skillet and add the cabbage. Cook over very low heat for about 30 minutes, stirring from time to time, until the cabbage is very soft and lightly colored. Add more fat if needed.

While the cabbage is cooking, boil the noodles in a large quantity of salted water for 10 to 12 minutes, until barely tender. Drain.

Add the noodles to the cabbage along with the caraway seeds, salt, pepper, and a pinch of sugar. Cover the pan and cook very slowly for 10 to 15 minutes. Taste for seasoning and serve. *Makes 6 to 8 servings.*

Rice Kugel (Pareve)

This dessert kugel is a turn on the basic idea of rice pudding, universal but here done without milk (to make it pareve), and with apples added for texture, flavor, and sweetness.

◆   ◆   ◆

2 tablespoons margarine, melted
1 1/2 cups uncooked rice
6 eggs
1/2 cup brown sugar
1/2 cup raisins
2 cups peeled and minced tart apples

Preheat the oven to 350 degrees. With a little of the margarine, brush the inside of a 2-quart charlotte mold.

Cook the rice in 4 quarts of lightly salted boiling water for 15 to 18 minutes, until very tender. Drain well.

Beat the eggs with the brown sugar until the mixture has increased to four or five times its original volume and is light beige in color, about 5 minutes in a standing electric mixer.

Stir in the rice and add the raisins, apples, and the remaining melted margarine. Turn the mixture into the greased mold and bake for 20 to 30 minutes, until the top is golden and the pudding is firm. Cool to room temperature before serving, or refrigerate and serve cold. *Makes 8 servings.*

Kasha

Kasha is a milled form of the old-fashioned grain buckwheat, which prospers in climates marginal or impossible for wheat. Kasha, with its nutty flavor, is one of my favorite starches.

◆　　　◆　　　◆

1 egg
1 cup whole roasted buckwheat groats (do not use medium or fine kasha)
Salt
2 cups chicken soup (see page 48) or water (or a combination of the two)
2 tablespoons shmaltz, butter, or margarine

Beat the egg in a small bowl just to combine the white and the yolk. Stir in the kasha and a pinch of salt.

Put the kasha in a heavy, ungreased frying pan—cast iron is best. Toast the groats over moderate heat until the grains separate and give off a nutty smell. Stir frequently from the bottom so they don't stick and burn.

In a heavy 2-quart saucepan with a lid, bring the chicken soup or water to a boil. Canned chicken stock will be saltier than homemade; if you use water, as much as 1/2 teaspoon salt might be necessary. Stir until salt is thoroughly dissolved. Slowly stir in the toasted groats. Add the fat. Tightly cover the saucepan (to trap the steam) and cook over the lowest possible heat until the liquid is absorbed, about 20 minutes. The kasha can also be cooked for the same amount of time in a preheated 325-degree oven. The grains should be dry and separate. You can fluff them with a fork and serve immediately or, if you have the time or want the kasha to wait, cover with a folded dishtowel, replace the lid, and keep warm in a 250-degree oven for several hours. *Makes 4 to 6 servings.*

Kasha Varnishkes

Kasha served with bowtie-shaped pasta. A classic.

◆　　　◆　　　◆

1 cup chopped onions
1 tablespoon shmaltz, butter, or margarine
1 cup (4 ounces) egg bowtie noodles
2 cups hot cooked kasha, prepared from 1 cup raw, as in preceding recipe

Slowly cook the onions in the fat for 15 to 20 minutes, until meltingly soft but not brown.

Meanwhile, boil the noodles in a large quantity of salted water for 10 minutes. Drain.

Combine the noodles, onions, and kasha in a large bowl and serve. If not to be eaten immediately, cover with a dishtowel and keep warm over very low heat for up to 1 hour. If a wait of several hours is needed, put the mixture in a greased ovenproof dish and reheat in a preheated 325-degree oven for about 20 minutes, until hot. *Makes 6 servings.*

MAMALIGA

This common Romanian form of cornmeal mush is identical to the polenta of northern Italy. Italian Jews use white cornmeal for it, to symbolize the purity of the Torah, when they make this dish on Shavuot, the early summer holiday that commemorates God's gift of the Law to Moses on Mount Sinai. If you make more than you need right away, you can bake or fry it later on (see recipes that follow).

◆   ◆   ◆

3 cups yellow or white cornmeal
2 tablespoons salt

Place the cornmeal in a medium bowl and stir in 2 cups cold water. Mash out any lumps with the side of a wooden spoon.

In a large heavy saucepan, bring 4 cups water and the salt to a boil. Gradually add the cornmeal, stirring constantly. Simmer for 10 minutes, stirring constantly to prevent sticking; the mixture will become very thick and hard to stir. Remove from the heat.

Dip a wooden spoon in cold water and push the cornmeal to the center of the pot. Put back over low heat for a minute or two, without stirring, to release steam and loosen the mixture from the bottom of the pan.

Turn the mamaliga out onto a board. Smooth the surface with a wet metal spatula, spreading the mixture to form a rectangle about 1 inch, or at most 2 inches, thick. The plain mamaliga can be served as is, cut into 1-inch squares. The traditional Romanian or Italian way of cutting the squares is with a taut string held between your thumbs and index fingers. Slip the string under the mamaliga and raise it quickly upward. This movement will cut the mamaliga in a clean line.

Served plain, mamaliga is a fine accompaniment to stews. It can also be eaten topped with cottage cheese, sour cream, yogurt, or grated cheese. If it is to be baked or fried, let it cool completely and solidify before using it in the recipes that follow. Plain mamaliga can be refrigerated for a day or two, or frozen. *Makes about 3 dozen 1-inch squares.*

Baked Mamaliga

Mamaliga (see opposite)
2 cups grated cheese
2 tablespoons butter or margarine

Preheat the oven to 375 degrees.

Cut cold mamaliga into strips 1/2 to 1 inch thick. In a casserole or gratin dish, layer the ingredients, starting with the mamaliga and ending with a layer of cheese and butter. Bake for about 30 minutes, until the cheese melts and the mamaliga is very hot throughout. *Makes 8 servings.*

Fried Mamaliga

Mamaliga (see opposite)
3 eggs, lightly beaten
3 cups grated Parmesan or romano cheese
2 tablespoons oil

Cut cold mamaliga into 2-inch squares. Dip the pieces in the beaten eggs and then in the cheese.

Heat the oil in a skillet and add the coated mamaliga. Fry until browned on both sides. Serve with sour cream or yogurt. *Makes 8 servings.*

POTATO LATKES

*P*otato pancakes are the traditional dish of Chanukah, the holiday that commemorates the recapture and rededication of the Temple by the Jewish military leader Judas Maccabaeus in 165 B.C. Since there were no potatoes available to any Jewish cook until the Spanish Conquest of Peru, some 1700 years later, it is definitely the oil that connects these tasty pancakes to Chanukah. They supplement the ritual of candlelighting which directly re-creates the miracle of the light in the Temple that would not fail during the eight days of crisis. The actual preparation of latkes is a matter of sophistication, debate, and—for the cook—devotion. Latkes take time and can't be made in advance. Disconnect any smoke alarms before heating the oil to fry them.

◆   ◆   ◆

6 *large Idaho potatoes, 8 to 9 ounces each,*
    peeled
3 *medium onions, peeled*
4 *eggs, lightly beaten to combine whites and*
    yolks
1/4 *to 1/2 cup all-purpose flour*
2 *to 3 tablespoons salt*
Freshly ground black pepper
Peanut oil for frying

Grate the potatoes using the largest holes on a 4-sided grater or, if using a processor, dice first and then process with the steel blade in spurts, to prevent producing a gluey purée. With each potato, grate or process half an onion.

Transfer the grated potatoes and onions to a sieve placed over a large bowl. Press out the excess moisture with a wooden spoon and transfer the vegetables to another bowl. Pour off all of the liquid from the first bowl, leaving behind the potato starch that settles at the bottom; add the starch to the grated potatoes and onions.

Beat the eggs into the potato-onion mixture. Then beat in just enough flour to make a light batter. Add salt and pepper.

Heat 1/4 inch of oil in a large heavy skillet. For each pancake, drop about 2 tablespoons of batter into the oil and flatten with the back of a wooden spoon; the flatter you make the pancakes, the crisper they will be. Some people prefer thicker pancakes with a soft interior. Fry for about 2 minutes on one side, then turn and fry for 30 seconds or so on the other side. Don't crowd the pan with too many pancakes, or else they will become soggy. Remove the finished pancakes with a spatula, drain them over the skillet, and place on paper towels. Keep the drained pancakes warm in a 200-degree oven while you fry the rest. Serve as soon as possible, with sour cream and/or applesauce (see page 126). *Makes about 40 3- to 4-inch latkes.*

Latkes. Some like them small and crisp, as here; others batten militantly on big, more potato-y pancakes.

Two Farfel Recipes

Farfel is made from egg noodle dough. It is available commercially as Barley Shape or Egg Barley, and sold either plain or toasted; if you can find only plain and prefer toasted, toast your own by spreading the farfel on a cookie sheet or in a shallow skillet and toasting it in a 350-degree oven for 15 to 20 minutes, tossing from time to time so that it browns evenly.

◆　　◆　　◆

Basic Farfel Recipe

2 cups egg barley, toasted or plain
Salt
2 cups chopped onions
3 tablespoons shmaltz or margarine
1 cup sliced mushrooms (optional)
Freshly ground black pepper

Boil the farfel in a large quantity of salted water for 10 minutes; drain.

Meanwhile, cook the onions very slowly in the shmaltz or margarine for 10 minutes or so, until they are very soft but not colored. Add the mushrooms, if you're using them, and cook for 7 minutes more. Add the farfel and season with salt and pepper to taste. *Makes 6 to 8 servings.*

Prune and Farfel Tsimmes

1 pound pitted prunes
1 1/2 cups egg barley, toasted or plain
Salt
2 tablespoons lemon juice
2 tablespoons honey
4 tablespoons margarine or butter

Soak the prunes in 2 cups of hot water or weak tea for 1 hour. Drain and coarsely chop the prunes, reserving the soaking liquid.

Preheat the oven to 350 degrees.

Cook the farfel in boiling salted water to cover for 8 minutes. Drain.

While the farfel is still hot, combine it with the prunes, lemon juice, honey, and margarine or butter. Transfer the mixture to a 1-quart gratin dish, cover with aluminum foil, and bake for 30 minutes. Remove the foil and bake for an additional 15 minutes. Serve hot. The tsimmes can also be reheated: cover and bake in a 300-degree oven for about 20 minutes. *Makes 6 servings.*

CHEESE BLINTZES

*B*lintzes are delicate pancakes rolled around a cheese filling and then fried. They are country cousins of Imperial Russian blinis and blinchiki, small crepes often made with buckwheat flour and served with caviar at the Winter Palace; they speak to one's higher earthly aspirations. Cheese blintzes fill the stomach on a cold Sunday morning, but they are traditional for Shavuot.

◆　　　◆　　　◆

PANCAKES

2 eggs
1 tablespoon unsalted butter, melted and cooled
1 cup unbleached flour
1/2 teaspoon salt
1 cup milk
1/4 teaspoon baking powder
Additional unsalted butter for frying

FILLING

1/2 pound farmer or pot cheese
2 ounces (4 tablespoons) cream cheese, at room
　temperature
1 egg, lightly beaten
1/2 tablespoon grated lemon peel
Salt

To make the pancakes, lightly beat the eggs in a bowl. Add the cooled melted butter, flour, salt, and milk. Stir until smooth. Add the baking powder.

Melt a teaspoon or so of butter in a 5- to 6-inch cast-iron skillet or nonstick pan. When the butter is hot, add 2 tablespoons of the batter and immediately rotate the pan to spread the batter evenly and thinly over the bottom; pour any excess back into the bowl. Cook for about 30 seconds on the first side. Slide the pancake onto a small plate and flip it back into the pan. Cook for about 15 seconds on the second side. Remove the pancake to a cookie sheet. Repeat with additional butter and the remaining batter. The cooked pancakes will keep for several hours at room temperature. This amount of batter will yield about 12 pancakes.

To make the filling, combine the farmer or pot cheese, cream cheese, egg, lemon peel, and a pinch of salt. Beat with a wooden spoon until smooth; press the filling through a sieve if it is lumpy.

To make the blintzes, put about 1 tablespoon of the filling in the center of each pancake. Roll sides and fold in the ends so the filling is completely enclosed. Heat butter in a large skillet and fry each blintz for about 4 minutes, turning to brown all sides. Serve immediately with sour cream. *Makes 6 servings.*

Note: blintzes can be frozen, either before or after frying. If they have been fried, defrost them before reheating in a 325-degree oven for about 20 minutes.

Vegetables and Fruits

◆ ◆ ◆

Eingemachts, preserved beets (page 107).

PICKLED BEETS

If you want to make a direct, sensuous connection with the life of the shtetl, spend an hour pickling beets. Then you will have also earned the right to eat them all winter and learn where Tevye got his lust for life.

◆　　　◆　　　◆

2 pounds beets
6 whole cloves
1 teaspoon allspice berries
2-inch stick cinnamon
2 cups white vinegar
1/2 cup sugar
2 cups sliced red onions

Leave about 1/2 inch of tail and 1 1/2 inches of stem on the beets. Wash gently under cold water; don't scrub the beets and try not to pierce them.

Place the beets in a steamer set in a large pot with an inch or two of water in the bottom. Bring to a boil, cover, and steam for 30 to 40 minutes. Add more boiling water to the pot if necessary. When done, the beets will feel tender to the touch. You can also boil the beets in simmering water to cover in a tightly covered pot for 30 to 60 minutes, depending on their size; or bake the beets in a 325-degree oven for about 1 hour. When the beets are cool enough to handle, slice off the stems and roots and slip off the skins.

Slice the beets and put them in a large saucepan. Tie the spices together in a wet cheesecloth bag and add to the beets along with the vinegar and sugar. Bring to a boil, lower the heat, and simmer for 5 minutes. Remove from heat. Add the onions. Let the beets cool in the liquid. Discard the spice bag and transfer the beets and onions and the liquid to a screw-top jar. Keep refrigerated. *Makes about 1 quart.*

EINGEMACHTS
BEET PRESERVES

*T*he Yiddish word *eingemachts* simply means preserves. And these are sweet beet preserves, an unusual accompaniment for meat dishes.

◆　　　◆　　　◆

4 pounds beets, cooked and peeled (see page 106)
8 cups sugar
2 lemons, sliced
2 tablespoons grated fresh ginger
1 cup chopped blanched almonds

Slice the beets into julienne strips or grate them coarsely. Put the beets in a large pot and add the sugar, lemon slices, ginger, and 3 cups of water.

Bring to a boil over low heat, stirring until the sugar dissolves. Simmer for about 2 hours, until the mixture is thick. Add the almonds and cook for 15 minutes more. Cool the eingemachts and store in the refrigerator, in screw-top jars. *Makes about 4 pints.*

HOT BEETS

6 to 8 cooked and peeled beets (see page 106)
2 tablespoons margarine
2 tablespoons chopped scallions, including some green tops
1 teaspoon sugar
1 tablespoon white vinegar
Salt
Freshly ground black pepper
1 tablespoon chopped parsley

Thinly slice the beets. In a saucepan over low heat, toss the beets with the margarine, scallions, sugar, vinegar, and salt and pepper. Just before serving, sprinkle with the parsley. *Makes 6 servings.*

OVERLEAF: *The fixings for red cabbage and apples (page 111).*

STUFFED CABBAGE (DAIRY)

When I went to Lyons in 1979 to report on the nouvelle cuisine in France for *Travel & Leisure* Magazine, the height of fashion in one restaurant in this gastronomic capital was to cook food in cabbage leaves. This would not have surprised my grandmother. She knew that a blanched and softened cabbage leaf could be an edible mold for almost any food. And she, like other Jews from the Russian Empire, had plenty of experience with cabbage, as this and the several cabbage recipes that follow demonstrate.

◆　　◆　　◆

One 2- to 2 1/2-pound green cabbage
3 cups thinly sliced onions
2 tablespoons butter or margarine
1 tablespoon brown sugar
2 tablespoons lemon juice
1 teaspoon grated lemon peel
1/4 teaspoon cinnamon
1 1/2 cups raisins
2 eggs
1 1/2 cups grated onions
2 cups rice, boiled for 6 minutes and drained, or
    2 cups kasha, cooked until barely done (see
    page 197)
Salt
Freshly ground black pepper
1 cup sour cream

Cut out the core of the cabbage and place the head in a large pot. Pour enough boiling water over the cabbage to cover it, put the lid on the pot, and set aside for about 15 minutes.

Meanwhile, slowly cook the sliced onions in the butter or margarine in a large heavy skillet until they are very soft but not brown. Add the brown sugar, lemon juice, lemon peel, cinnamon, and 1/2 cup of the raisins.

Remove the cabbage from the hot water. Peel off the leaves, one by one, without tearing them. If any leaves still seem stiff, put them back in the pot and bring the water to a boil. Remove the leaves after 2 or 3 minutes; they must be limp enough to fold around the stuffing without tearing. With a small sharp knife, shave off the hard ribs. The center leaves of the cabbage are too small to stuff; shred these leaves and add them to the onions. If the outermost leaves are very large, cut them in half.

To make the stuffing, lightly beat the eggs, and add the grated onions, partially cooked rice or kasha, remaining raisins, and salt and pepper. Place a spoonful or two of this mixture on each cabbage leaf. Fold the leaves to completely enclose the filling.

One by one, placed the stuffed cabbage leaves in the skillet with the onions. Add enough water to come about one third of the way up the cabbage rolls. Cover and cook very gently for about 2 hours.

Remove the stuffed cabbage to a serving platter. Beat the sour cream for a moment or two in a medium bowl. Beat the hot liquid from the cabbage into the sour cream 2 or 3 tablespoons at a time. Then pour it back into the pan and stir to combine with the onions and raisins. Pour the sauce over the stuffed cabbage leaves and serve. *Makes 18 to 22 stuffed cabbage leaves; serves 10 to 12 as an appetizer or 6 to 8 as an entrée.*

Sweet and Sour Cabbage

One 2-pound green cabbage, tough outer leaves
    removed
Salt
2 tablespoons brown sugar
3 tablespoons lemon juice
2/3 cup raisins
Freshly ground black pepper

Halve, core, and coarsely shred the cabbage.
Combine the cabbage, 1 tablespoon salt,
and 1/2 cup water in a large enameled pan.
Bring to a boil, cover, and simmer gently for
20 to 30 minutes.

Add the brown sugar, lemon juice, and
raisins. Re-cover the pot and cook gently for
another 15 to 20 minutes, until the cabbage
is tender. Taste for seasoning and add more
sugar, lemon juice, salt, or pepper, as needed. *Makes 6 to 8 servings.*

Red Cabbage and Apples

One 1 1/2-pound red cabbage, halved, cored,
    and roughly shredded (about 6 cups)
4 tablespoons margarine, butter, or vegetable oil
2 to 2 1/2 cups chopped onions
1 pound tart apples, peeled, cored, and coarsely
    chopped
2 teaspoons caraway seeds
Salt
Freshly ground black pepper

Cover the shredded cabbage with boiling
water and let stand for 15 minutes. Drain.

Heat the fat in a large skillet and cook
the onions until they are very soft but not
colored. Add the apples, cabbage, caraway
seeds, and salt and pepper. Cover the skillet
and cook over very low heat for about 45
minutes, until the cabbage and apples are
soft. *Makes 6 to 8 servings.*

COLE SLAW

What makes this a Jewish dish? 1) Jews in Europe ate it and continue to eat it. 2) It has sour cream in it, and no goyish coleslaw in the United States can make that claim.

◆　　　◆　　　◆

One 1 1/2-pound green cabbage, cored and
　　shredded
Kosher salt
1 carrot, scraped
1/2 green bell pepper
1 celery stalk
1/2 cup sour cream
2 tablespoons mayonnaise
1 tablespoon lemon juice
1 1/2 teaspoon sugar

Place the cabbage in a colander, sprinkle generously with kosher salt, and let stand for 15 to 20 minutes.

Shred the carrot on a coarse grater. Cut the green pepper into 1-inch strips and slice the strips crosswise into 1/4-inch pieces. Cut the celery into 1/4-inch slices.

Wash the cabbage in cold water and drain thoroughly. Pat dry with paper towels.

In the bowl in which you plan to serve the coleslaw, combine the sour cream, mayonnaise, lemon juice, and sugar. Beat until blended. Add the prepared vegetables and mix well. Taste for seasoning. *Makes 6 servings.*

NAHIT
CHICKPEAS

Chickpeas are traditionally served on the Friday following the birth of a child, as well as at Purim (the Spring holiday that commemorates Queen Esther's rescue of the Jews from decimation by the evil courtier Haman in the royal court of Shushan, Persia).

◆　　　◆　　　◆

2 cups dried chickpeas
Salt
Freshly ground black pepper

Wash and pick over the chickpeas. Soak them overnight in water to cover; drain.

Place the chickpeas in a large saucepan with cold water to cover and bring to a boil. Add salt, and simmer until tender, anywhere from 1 to 3 hours, depending on the freshness of the beans. Add boiling water from time to time to keep the beans covered.

Drain the beans and dry well with paper towels. Place in a serving bowl and sprinkle with salt and pepper. Refrigerate until ready to serve. *Makes 4 servings.*

Dried chickpeas, a staple starch in the Mediterranean that Jews brought with them as they traveled north and east.

Honeyed Carrots

*2 pounds carrots (12-16 medium), scraped and
sliced into 1/2-inch rounds*
1/4 cup orange juice
Salt
1/4 cup honey
4 tablespoons margarine or butter

Combine all of the ingredients in a heavy
saucepan and add 2 tablespoons of water.
Cover and cook over very low heat for about
25 minutes, until the carrots are tender and
the liquid is syrupy. *Makes 6 to 8 servings.*

Peas and Carrots

1/2 cup minced onions
4 tablespoons butter or margarine
*1 pound carrots, scraped and cut into thin
rounds*
1 teaspoon sugar
*1/2 pound shelled fresh or frozen peas (about
2 cups)*

Gently cook the onions in the butter or
margarine until softened. Add the carrots,
sugar, and 1/4 cup of water. Cover and cook
gently for 10 to 12 minutes, until the carrots
are just tender. Add the peas and cook for an
additional 2 minutes. *Makes 6 servings.*

Mushrooms and Sour Cream

1/2 cup minced onions
3 tablespoons butter
1 pound mushrooms, sliced
Salt
Freshly ground black pepper
1/2 teaspoon paprika
3/4 cup sour cream

Slowly cook the onions in 1 1/2 tablespoons butter until they are very soft but not brown. Remove from the pan and reserve.

Cook the mushrooms in the same pan in the remaining butter for about 10 minutes, until most of their liquid has evaporated.

Stir in the reserved onions, salt, pepper, and the paprika and cook for about 5 minutes. Add the sour cream and serve spooned over toast. *Makes 4 to 6 servings.*

Stuffed Peppers (dairy)

6 small green bell peppers
1 pound pot cheese
1 cup finely chopped scallions, including green tops
1 zucchini, finely chopped
2 eggs, lightly beaten
Salt
Freshly ground black pepper

Preheat the oven to 350 degrees.

Slice off the tops of the peppers and remove the cores. Place the peppers in a large saucepan with cold water to cover. Bring to a boil and cook for 5 minutes; drain. Carefully remove the ribs and seeds without puncturing the peppers (a grapefruit knife is the tool of choice for this job).

Combine the remaining ingredients in a bowl and use this mixture to stuff the peppers. Stand the peppers upright in a 3-inch-deep soufflé dish or other ovenproof casserole that will hold them snugly. Pour about 1/2 inch of water into the dish and bake for 30 minutes, until the peppers are tender. Serve warm or at room temperature. *Makes 6 servings.*

Food wrapped or stuffed in other food is a method of cooking popular from Mexico (tamales) to Manchuria (steamed dumplings). At one end of the spectrum is blood pudding (coagulated pork blood in a casing of pork intestine). At the other end is this kosher, vegetarian invention, in which a conveniently hollow vegetable holds and protects the nonmeat forcemeat.

MUSHROOM SHNITZEL

As the name indicates, this is a mock meat dish. Jews have a special impetus to cook such foods because they permit the semblance of meat in the middle of a dairy meal where real meat is forbidden. Several other vegetarian dishes follow this one.

◆   ◆   ◆

1 cup minced scallions, including some green
    tops
1 cup minced onions
12 tablespoons butter or margarine
1 1/2 pounds mushrooms, finely chopped
1 tablespoon minced parsley
2 eggs, lightly beaten
⅓ cup matzo meal, approximately
Salt
Freshly ground black pepper

Cook the scallions and onions in 6 tablespoons butter or margarine until soft. Add the mushrooms and sauté over moderately high heat for 10 to 15 minutes, until all of their liquid has evaporated. Turn into a mixing bowl and let cool.

Add the parsley, eggs, and, gradually, the matzo meal; the mixture should have enough body to hold together during frying. Add another tablespoon or two of matzo meal if necessary. Season with salt and pepper.

Heat the remaining butter or margarine in a large heavy skillet. To form each shnitzel, place 1 heaping tablespoon of the mushroom mixture in the hot fat and spread with the back of a wooden spoon to a diameter of about 3 inches and fry until lightly browned on both sides. You can also make smaller shnitzels to serve as hors d'oeuvres. As the shnitzels are done, drain on paper towels. Serve with lemon wedges or sour cream. *Makes 20 to 24 mushroom shnitzels.*

Vegetable Cutlets

1 cup chopped onions
1/2 cup chopped celery
1 cup grated carrots
2 tablespoons butter or margarine
1/2 cup coarsely chopped, parboiled green beans
1/2 cup shelled peas, cooked for 1 minute
3 eggs
1/2 cup matzo meal, approximately
Salt
Freshly ground black pepper
Vegetable oil for frying

Cook the onions, celery, and carrots in the butter or margarine for 10 minutes. Transfer to a mixing bowl.

Add the cooked beans and peas, 2 of the eggs, and 6 tablespoons of the matzo meal. Combine well and season with salt and pepper. Add 1 or 2 more tablespoons matzo meal if the mixture seems too loose to hold together during frying—it should shape easily into cutlets.

Beat the remaining egg on a plate and spread 2 tablespoons of the matzo meal on another plate. Using a scant 1/4 cup for each cutlet, shape the vegetable mixture into disks. Dip each cutlet first in matzo meal and then in beaten egg.

Meanwhile, heat the oil. Add the vegetable cutlets and fry until lightly browned on both sides. Drain on paper towels and serve. *Makes 12 cutlets.*

Vegetable Loaf

3 tablespoons shmaltz or margarine
1 cup chopped onions
1 cup chopped celery
1 cup grated carrots
1 to 1 1/2 cups coarsely chopped mushrooms
    (1/4 pound)
1 cup chopped walnuts
1/4 pound green beans
Salt
3 eggs
1 cup bread crumbs
Freshly ground black pepper

Preheat the oven to 350 degrees. Grease a 9x5-inch loaf pan.

Heat the shmaltz or margarine in a heavy medium skillet. Add the onions and cook slowly until softened. Add the celery, carrots, mushrooms, and walnuts to the skillet and cook for 15 minutes.

Snap the ends off the green beans and parboil them for 2 minutes in a large quantity of boiling water. Add salt to the water after the beans have been added; this will set their color. Drain and cut the beans into thirds.

Lightly beat the eggs in a large mixing bowl. Add the cooked vegetables, green beans, bread crumbs, and salt and pepper. Mix well and stir in 3/4 cup water. Turn the mixture into the prepared loaf pan and bake for 45 minutes, until all the liquid is absorbed. Serve hot, in slices. *Makes 4 to 6 servings.*

ABOVE: *With mushroom and barley soup (page 45), as with vegetable loaf (page 119), Jewish hunger triumphs over the agricultural limitations of the Russian empire.*

RIGHT: *In dishes like this carrot ring (page 122), the polite baking of another era survives in our time and place.*

CARROT RING

1 1/2 pounds carrots, scraped and sliced into
    thin rounds
1 cup brown sugar
1 1/2 cups solid vegetable shortening
4 eggs, separated
2 1/2 cups all-purpose flour
2 teaspoons baking soda
1 teaspoon baking powder
1 teaspoon salt
3 tablespoons lemon juice
1 teaspoon grated lemon peel
1 teaspoon almond extract

Cook the carrots in a large quantity of boiling salted water for 15 to 20 minutes, until
very tender. Drain well. Purée the carrots in
a blender or processor.

Preheat the oven to 350 degrees and
grease an 8-cup ring mold.

Cream together the brown sugar and
shortening. Add the egg yolks and the carrot
purée.

Sift the flour with the baking soda, baking powder, and salt. Add to the carrot mixture alternately with the lemon juice, lemon
peel, almond extract, and 2 tablespoons
water.

Beat the egg whites until stiff but not dry.
Fold them into the carrot mixture, then gently turn the mixture into the prepared ring
mold. Bake for 50 minutes to 1 hour, until
the ring has puffed and the top is slightly
cracked and lightly colored. Invert the ring
onto a serving dish and serve hot or at room
temperature. *Makes 6 to 8 servings.*

POTATO AND PARSNIP KUGEL

What is a kugel? In standard German, a kugel is a ball or sphere, sometimes a bullet. In a Jewish kitchen, it is a kind of baked pudding. There are many kugels in Jewish cookery. You will find others on pages 92-93 and 146-147.

◆   ◆   ◆

3 pounds potatoes, quartered
1 pound parsnips, scraped and quartered
5 tablespoons shmaltz or margarine
3 cups coarsely chopped onions
3 eggs, lightly beaten
Salt
Freshly ground black pepper
Nutmeg
1 tablespoon matzo meal

Boil the potatoes in their skins with the
parsnips for 20 minutes, until both are
tender. Drain well.

Meanwhile, heat 3 tablespoons shmaltz
or margarine in a skillet. Add the onions
and cook for 15 to 20 minutes, until very
soft and translucent.

Preheat the oven to 400 degrees.

When the potatoes are cool enough to
handle, peel them and mash in a large bowl
together with the parsnips. Mix in the eggs
and onions. Season generously with salt,
pepper, and a few gratings of nutmeg.

Grease a 2 1/2- to 3-quart casserole or
gratin dish with the remaining shmaltz or
margarine and sprinkle with the matzo meal.
Add the potato mixture and bake 45 to 60
minutes, until the top is golden. *Makes 8 to
10 servings.*

Vegetable and Dried Fruit Tsimmes

A tsimmes is a stew or casserole containing dried fruit (see page 72 for a tsimmes with meat). But there is also a Yiddish idiom, "to make a tsimmes out of" (machen a tsimmes fun . . .), which means to make a big deal out of something. In general, this idiom has a negative coloring to it, just as does the American expression, "to make a federal case" out of something. But in the kitchen, to make a tsimmes, a literal tsimmes, is to create a bona fide big deal with lots of peeling and chopping. But perhaps there's no need to make such a tsimmes out of what is really a simple, yet inspired, food idea.

◆   ◆   ◆

10 large carrots, scraped and cut into 1-inch slices
2 pounds sweet potatoes, peeled and cut into 1-inch dice
1/2 cup pitted prunes
1/4 cup chopped pitted dates
1/4 cup honey
1/4 teaspoon cinnamon
1/4 teaspoon nutmeg
1 1/2 teaspoons grated orange peel
1 cup orange juice
1 tablespoon butter or margarine

Cook the carrots and sweet potatoes in boiling water to cover for 10 minutes, until barely tender. Drain.

Preheat the oven to 350 degrees.

Combine the carrots and sweet potatoes with all of the remaining ingredients except the butter or margarine. Turn the mixture into a shallow 3-quart baking dish. Dot the top with the butter or margarine and bake for 30 minutes. If the top becomes too brown, cover with foil. *Makes 8 servings.*

ABOVE: *Ingredients for vegetable and dried-fruit tsimmes (page 123). Clockwise: carrots, honey, chopped dates, grated orange peel, nutmeg, prunes, and sweet potatoes.*

RIGHT: *A finished tsimmes.*

BAKED APPLES

6 large tart apples
2 tablespoons butter or margarine
2 tablespoons sugar combined with 1 teaspoon
    cinnamon (or 2 tablespoons honey with no
    cinnamon)
1 cup apple cider or water

Preheat the oven to 350 degrees.

Core the apples with a grapefruit knife, being careful not to cut all the way through from top to bottom.

Put the apples in a shallow baking dish or roasting pan. Place 1 teaspoon of the butter or margarine in each apple and then add the cinnamon sugar or the honey and sugar.

Pour the apple juice or water into the pan and bake, basting the apples occasionally, for 30 to 45 minutes, until the apples are tender. Serve warm, at room temperature, or chilled, with heavy cream. *Makes 6 servings.*

APPLESAUCE

4 pounds tart apples (McIntosh, Cortland,
    Northern Spy)
1/2 cup apple juice, apple cider, or water
Peel of 1 lemon, removed in large strips with a
    vegetable peeler
1/4 to 1/2 cup sugar
1/8 to 1/2 teaspoon cinnamon
Nutmeg
Lemon juice

Quarter and core the apples; don't peel them. Place the apples in a heavy saucepan. Add the apple juice (or cider or water) and the lemon peel. Cover the pan and cook over very low heat, stirring from time to time, for about 30 minutes, until the apples are tender.

Put the apples in a food mill set over a large bowl. Purée the apples, discarding the skins and the lemon peel.

Return the purée to the saucepan and add sugar, cinnamon, and a few grindings of nutmeg, as you think necessary. The applesauce might be delicious just as it is. Cook the applesauce very slowly, uncovered, until it is thick. Taste again for seasoning, adding more sugar and a sprinkling of lemon juice, if necessary. *Makes 4 cups.*

DRIED FRUIT COMPOTE

*I*n a world where fresh fruit was scarce at almost all times, dried fruit came to occupy a central place in the making of desserts. The compote is a dodge that permits dried fruit to be reconstituted in advance of use and then stored. This recipe makes a virtue out of necessity. So does the recipe for stewed prunes which follows.

◆　　　◆　　　◆

5 pounds mixed dried fruits (prunes, apricots, apples, pears), or prunes only
2 cups white wine
1 cup sugar
1 lemon, quartered
1 cinnamon stick
Lemon juice

Put the fruit in a large saucepan and add the wine, sugar, lemon quarters, cinnamon, and 2 cups of water. Bring to a boil, lower the heat, and simmer very gently for about 30 minutes, until the fruit is tender. Remove from the heat and let the fruit cool in the saucepan. Taste to determine if the mixture needs more sugar or lemon juice. Store the fruit and its syrup in a tightly covered jar in the refrigerator. The compote will keep for weeks. *Makes 12 to 14 servings.*

STEWED PRUNES

1 pound pitted unsweetened prunes
1/2 cinnamon stick
1/2 lemon, sliced
Sugar, if necessary

In a heavy pot, soak the prunes for several hours or overnight in warm water to cover.

Add the cinnamon stick, lemon slices, and enough additional water to barely cover the prunes. Bring to a simmer and cook gently for 15 minutes. Taste and add sugar, if necessary. Remove the prunes to a heat-proof bowl and boil down the liquid to a fairly thick syrup. Pour the hot syrup over the prunes and let cool before refrigerating in a screw-top jar.

An alternate way of cooking the prunes is to put them in a heatproof bowl with the cinnamon and lemon and pour over boiling water to cover. Cover the bowl and let sit overnight. *Makes 6 servings.*

CHAPTER

8

Salads

♦ ♦ ♦

One way to define a cuisine is to notice the foods it does not include. Jewish food that comes to us from Eastern Europe is not rich in green vegetables, to say the least, and the typical salads of the cuisine are all but devoid of lettuce. It is easy to guess why. And one has only to make a tour of Russian markets today to confirm that guess. The growing season is short in those latitudes, and traditional agriculture has stressed ingredients that could be stored through the long winter. But sweet are the uses of adversity. The salads that Ashkenazis brought with them are an ingenious, distinct, and delicious alternative to the fresh, raw greens we usually eat today.

Herring salad (page 130).

HERRING SALAD

*P*ickled herring is the principal fish of Jewish cooking. Here is a light, chaste version in which apple and onion counterpoint the tartness of the fish with a mild sweet note.

◆   ◆   ◆

1 pound pickled herring fillets
2 hard-boiled eggs
1 small tart apple, peeled
1 small onion, peeled
1 tablespoon lemon juice
1 tablespoon vegetable oil
Pinch of sugar

Soak the herring fillets in cold water for 20 to 30 minutes. Rinse and pat dry. Dice the fillets.

Chop the herring and eggs together as fine as possible. Transfer to a mixing bowl and grate in the apple and onion. Add the lemon juice, oil, and sugar. Refrigerate for at least 30 minutes before serving with crackers, matzos, or toast. *Makes 2 cups.*

HERRING AND POTATO SALAD

*P*ickled herring and sour cream is a universally loved combination of preserved fish and preserved cream. In this variation, scallions and celery contribute crunch to the basic soft texture of the dish.

◆   ◆   ◆

1 pound pickled herring fillets
3 cups peeled and diced boiled potatoes (about 2 pounds)
1/4 cup minced scallions, including some green tops
1 cup diced celery
1/2 cup sour cream
1 tablespoon lemon juice
2 tablespoons minced parsley

Rinse, dry, and dice the herring. Combine with the remaining ingredients. *Makes 6 to 8 servings.*

Cucumber Salad

2 large cucumbers, peeled and halved lengthwise
1/3 cup minced scallions, including some green
  tops
1/4 cup white vinegar or lemon juice
Pinch of sugar
Freshly ground black pepper

Scoop out and discard the cucumber seeds. Coarsely chop the cucumbers. Place in a serving bowl and combine with the remaining ingredients. Chill before serving. *Makes 4 servings.*

Beet Salad

*H*ere is my favorite of all these salads. Bland, solid, earthy beets are enlivened with a mayonnaise spiked with horseradish, mustard, sour cream, and scallions.

◆   ◆   ◆

7 to 8 medium beets, cooked and peeled (see
  page 106)
1/4 cup sour cream
1/2 teaspoon prepared white horseradish
1/2 teaspoon Dijon mustard
2 tablespoons mayonnaise
2 tablespoons minced scallions, including some
  green tops
2 tablespoons chopped parsley or dill

Slice, dice, or chop the beets. Place all of the remaining ingredients (except for the parsley or dill) in a serving bowl, add the beets, and mix gently but well. Refrigerate for 1 to 2 hours. Before serving, sprinkle with the parsley or dill. *Makes 6 to 8 servings.*

OVERLEAF: *Three salads. From top, clockwise: beet and cucumber (page 134), cucumber salad, and beet salad.*

Beet and Cucumber Salad

3 cucumbers, peeled, seeded, and cubed
2 tablespoons kosher salt
6 to 8 medium beets, cooked and peeled (see page 106)
1/2 cup chopped scallions, including green tops
1 tablespoon lemon juice
1 cup sour cream

Place the cucumbers in a colander and sprinkle with the salt. Let stand for 30 minutes. Rinse well. Dry the cucumbers with paper towels.

Cube the beets and place in a serving bowl. Add the scallions, lemon juice, sour cream, and cucumbers. Mix well and chill before serving. *Makes 6 to 8 servings.*

Potato Salad

*T*he sour cream gives this potato salad its Eastern European flavor.

◆   ◆   ◆

2 to 2 1/2 pounds potatoes
2 tablespoons white vinegar
1 cup chopped celery
1/2 cup chopped scallions, including some green tops
1/2 cup diced green bell pepper
1/4 cup minced parsley
1/2 cup mayonnaise
1/4 sour cream or yogurt
Salt
Freshly ground black pepper

Boil the potatoes in their skins until tender but not falling apart. Drain, peel, and quarter or cut them into eighths. While the potatoes are still warm, mix with the vinegar.

Add the celery, scallions, green pepper, and parsley. Stir in the mayonnaise and sour cream or yogurt. Season with salt and pepper. *Makes 6 to 8 servings.*

HEALTH SALAD

What makes it healthy? Because I say so; because everyone always has said so. Tradition, tradition. Anyway, what could it hurt? And the mix of shredded cabbage, carrots, and bell pepper is an appealing variation on coleslaw—without oil or egg yolks to boost the calorie and cholesterol counts. You see, healthy.

◆　　　◆　　　◆

One 2-pound green cabbage
2 tablespoons kosher salt
2 green bell peppers, cored, seeded, and diced
1 1/2 cups chopped scallions, including green
　　tops
2 carrots, scraped and shredded or sliced into
　　thin rounds
1 cup white or cider vinegar
2 tablespoons sugar

Discard the tough outer leaves of the cabbage, then halve and core it. Shred the cabbage and place it in a colander set over a bowl. Add the salt and mix well with your hands. Let stand for 30 minutes. Rinse the cabbage and drain.

In a large serving bowl, mix together the peppers, scallions, carrots, and cabbage. Add the vinegar and sugar. Mix well. Refrigerate for a few hours before serving. *Makes 8 to 10 servings.*

GARDEN SALAD

This is the *ne plus ultra* of dairy salads—crisp radishes and cucumber in sour cream-smoothed cottage cheese. For a lighter, tarter variation, substitute yogurt for the cottage cheese and sour cream.

◆　　　◆　　　◆

1 large cucumber
10 radishes, trimmed and sliced
6 scallions, including green tops, trimmed and
　　chopped
1/2 cup chopped green bell pepper
2 cups cottage cheese (1 pound)
1 cup sour cream
Freshly ground black pepper

Peel the cucumber if it's been waxed, and dice it. Combine all of the vegetables with the cottage cheese. Pass the sour cream separately, along with a pepper mill. Alternatively, serve the chopped vegetables, cottage cheese, and sour cream in separate bowls and let each diner make his own salad. *Makes 4 to 6 servings.*

CHAPTER
━━━━━━━◆━━━━━━━

9

Passover

◆　　◆　　◆

Passover (Pesach) is the culinary high point of the Jewish ritual year. The holiday celebration, which occupies a full week in spring roughly at the time of Christian Holy Week and Easter, centers around two identical meals called Seders (the Last Supper was a Seder).

The Seder begins and ends as a religious service conducted at the family table. In miniature, and with abundant gastronomic symbolism, it commemorates the flight from Egypt and the deliverance of the Jewish people from Pharaoh's oppressive rule. In all of Jewish worship, there is nothing to compare with the Seder in its complexity of reference and resonant density of observance. For this reason, the Seder requires its own prayer book, the Haggadah. And the special rules of Passover kashruth literally turn a pious home upside down.

It boils down to this: Passover is a gastronomic holiday whose main point is to teach children about the privation of flight and exile. The protracted preprandial service forces the young to sit and be hungry, to experience directly the pangs their ancestors felt in the desert. During that service, they are from time to time allowed to consume small

The traditional seder plate with its symbolic foods (from top, clockwise):
horseradish, parsley, roasted egg, celery leaves, lamb shank, and haroset (page 140).

amounts of wine and symbolic anti-foods—salt water and horseradish and haroset (chopped fruits and nuts)—culinary eccentricities never eaten at any other time in quite this way, even during the Passover week. For an hour or so, the children wait and listen to an incomprehensibly scholastic and nonnarrative analysis of the historical events described in the book of Exodus. They grow hungry and then they are fed a very full meal, but a meal which is itself circumscribed by a set of prohibitions unique to the occasion.

So there are two systems of paradox at work. The first is that of the anti-meal of the service; the second is that of the special dietary restrictions of the Passover meal itself. The first paradox—the service of the Haggadah—is an object lesson in history taught through mortification of the flesh and a subversion of normal eating. This service is a fast in the form of a meal. The second paradox of the Seder embodies an even more fundamental paradox. It is the opposition between normal eating, whose most basic act is the consumption of bread, and the special festivities of the Seder, whose basic act is the consumption of unleavened anti-bread, matzo.

Matzo is called the bread of affliction. It is flat and unleavened by yeast fermentation because the Jews in their haste to flee Egypt did not have time to wait for dough to rise. This is the legend, and Exodus 12:15 turned that legend into a dietary prohibition against risen loaves on Passover: "Seven days shall ye eat unleavened bread; even the first day ye shall put away leaven out of your houses: for whosoever eateth leavened bread from the first day until the seventh day, that soul shall be cut off from Israel."

The commandment is clear, and the faithful apply it with great thoroughness. By nine in the morning on the day of the first Seder, they have purged their homes of every speck of food from the past year because it could be contaminated with bread or bread crumbs. During Passover, even foods that resemble bread or flour are forbidden. This category is called chametz. It includes five grains: wheat, barley, spelt, rye, and oats. Ashkenazic commentators added rice to this list as well as the kitniyot: beans, peas, lentils, corn, maize, millet, mustard, and other legumes (but not their oils and other derivative liquid products). Sephardic Jews do not forbid rice or the kitniyot at Passover.

In effect, the prohibition against chametz makes matzo the only permissible grain product in Jewish homes for an entire week. This deprivation has had the paradoxical effect of inspiring a mini-cuisine of special dishes built around matzo itself and around matzo meal, a pseudo-flour that substitutes for forbidden real flour. As the recipes in this chapter demonstrate, every major category of baking has its special Passover counterpart, cobbled together brilliantly either from matzo meal or ground nuts.

At the heart of this food-obsessed asceticism is matzo itself. A flat, corrugated cracker, matzo can be made with or without eggs. It is even sometimes covered with chocolate. The very pious exercise fanatical care in watching over the purity of the milling of the flour to make sure it is not contaminated. But the fundamental recipe—invariably baked by professionals in our day—is utterly simple. Flour and water are mixed, the dough is rolled out flat and then it is baked until lightly browned. All this must be done within 18 minutes after the flour is moistened. After 18 minutes have passed, the rabbis reason, airborne yeast or yeast somehow present in the flour would have time to begin fermenting in the presence of flour and water, making matzo into chametz. Observant Jews take the various restrictions of Passover in stride and, more than that, take pleasure in the special character of the Seder dishes. They know why "this night is different from all other nights" and they have learned to enjoy that difference.

◆　　　　◆　　　　◆

Haroset

The Seder table is set with various ceremonial foods: matzo, a lamb shank, a roasted egg, parsley, salt water, horseradish, and haroset. I was taught that haroset resembled the bricks and mortar that Jews in slavery to Pharaoh were forced to work with. Ashkenazi use apples. Sephardi use dates.

◆   ◆   ◆

Ashkenazic Haroset

1 pound tart apples, peeled and cored
4 ounces walnut halves (1 to 1 1/4 cups)
3/4 tablespoon cinnamon
3 to 5 tablespoons sweet wine

Finely chop the apples and walnuts. Add the cinnamon and mix together in a bowl. Add enough wine to moisten and create a paste-like texture. Taste and add more cinnamon if necessary. *Makes 4 cups.*

Sephardic Haroset I

1/2 pound pitted dates (1 cup packed down)
4 ounces walnut pieces (1 cup)
6 to 8 tablespoons sweet wine

Chop the dates and nuts and combine in a bowl. Add the wine by tablespoons until a pastelike mixture is achieved. Refrigerate for at least 1 hour before serving. *Makes 1 1/2 cups.*

Sephardic Haroset II

1/2 pound pitted dates (1 cup packed down)
1/2 cup raisins
1 medium apple, peeled, cored, and chopped
2 ounces walnut pieces (1/2 cup)
1 teaspoon freshly grated ginger
1/4 cup sweet wine

Combine all the ingredients except the wine, and chop fine. Alternatively, chop with just a few quick pulses in a food processor. Stir in the wine to make a pastelike mixture. *Makes 2 cups.*

Ingredients for Sephardic haroset II (clockwise):
dates, wine, walnuts, raisins, apple, ginger, and cinnamon.

CHRAIN
HORSERADISH

1 horseradish root, about 4 inches long
White vinegar or lemon juice

Peel the horseradish and grate it using the fine side of a grater, or finely shred it in a processor. If you want to keep the horseradish, sprinkle it with vinegar or lemon juice and store in a covered jar in the refrigerator. For serving immediately, there's no need to add the vinegar. *Makes about 1 cup.*

CHRAIN WITH BEETS

2 medium beets, cooked and peeled (see page 106)
1 horseradish root, about 4 inches long
2 to 4 tablespoons wine, white vinegar, or cider vinegar
2 teaspoons kosher salt
1 teaspoon sugar

Grate the beets into a bowl using the fine side of a hand grater. Finely grate the horseradish into the bowl. Add the wine or vinegar, salt, and sugar. Taste for seasoning. Let stand at room temperature for 2 hours before serving. Stored covered in the refrigerator, the chrain will keep for several weeks. *Makes 1 1/2 cups.*

GEFILTE FISH

*T*his is a family recipe for the fish dumplings that are the Jewish cook's answer to France's *quenelles de brochet*. Pike is common to both preparations and so is the basic method of grinding fish, binding it with other ingredients, and then poaching it. Gefilte fish is the traditional first course of the Seder meal in Ashkenazic homes. Horseradish is the traditional accompaniment.

The combination of fish listed here is only a suggestion. In other families, other proportions are insisted on. One thing is certain: there is no fish called gefilte (the word means "stuffed" and refers to an obsolete form of the recipe). But the idea that there is such a fish inspired the single funniest bit of television news I have ever witnessed. Late in the 1960s, on New York City local news, Heywood Hale Broun narrated a tongue-in-cheek feature on the demise of the gefilte in local waters. It was a brilliant satire on environmentalist scare bulletins. Broun went so far as to film fishermen sitting on docks with their feet up, sagely complaining that they hadn't seen a gefilte in months.

◆   ◆   ◆

2 pounds whitefish
2 pounds yellow pike
1 pound carp
3 medium onions, peeled and sliced
1/4 cup salt
2 tablespoons sugar
2 tablespoons matzo meal
3 eggs, lightly beaten
3 to 4 carrots, scraped and cut into rounds
Freshly ground white or black pepper
3 packages unflavored gelatin, if necessary

Ask your fishmonger to fillet the fish, reserving the bones and heads for you; ask also for an extra head—it will improve the broth.

Coarsely grind the fish with 2 of the onions in a meat grinder or processor. Transfer the mixture to a wooden bowl and continue chopping with a mezzaluna (half-moon–shaped chopper) as you work in 2 tablespoons salt, 1 tablespoon sugar, the matzo meal, eggs, and enough water (about 1/4 cup) to produce a smooth, light paste. If you don't have a mezzaluna, you can do this on a cutting board with a knife. Either way, make a well in the center of the mixture before adding the eggs and water.

Put the fish heads and bones into a large wide pot along with the carrots, pepper, and the remaining 2 tablespoons salt, 1 tablespoon sugar, and 1 onion. Cover with plenty of water and bring to a boil.

In a separate pot, bring 3 quarts of water to a boil.

When the first pot comes to a boil, prepare the fish balls. Keeping your hands moist with cold water, form spheres the size of very large eggs (they will expand when cooked) and drop them, one by one, into the pot with the fish bones. The water should be kept at a slow simmer as you continue to add fish balls. After all the balls have been added, simmer for 1 1/2 hours. Add additional water from the second pot as necessary, so that there is enough liquid to keep the balls afloat. Remove from the heat and let the fish balls cool in their liquid.

With a slotted spoon, remove the fish balls to a serving platter. Strain the cooking liquid. Pour it into a large jar and refrigerate until cold. It should gel. If it doesn't, rewarm the liquid and dissolve 1 package of gelatin in it. Test by putting a teaspoon of the liquid on a plate and refrigerating; if it doesn't gel, add more gelatin (up to 3 packages) until it does. Refrigerate until chilled.

Serve the fish cold, with the fish aspic and chrain. *Makes 8 to 10 servings.*

LEFT: *Preparing to make gefilte fish (page 143),
with (from top) yellow pike, carp, whitefish.*

ABOVE: *Gefilte fish. Drain, cool, and serve.*

THREE PASSOVER KUGELS

At the most general level kugel is a pudding made of starch smoothed out with fat and seasoned with spices and—usually—onions. At Pesach time it was natural for cooks to add matzo to the starch component of kugels. And, for a sweet kugel, fruit and nuts take the place of onions.

◆   ◆   ◆

MATZO FARFEL KUGEL

Matzo farfel is what you might call Passover pasta. The farfel are small, manufactured noodlettes shaped like barley. They lend themselves to making baked puddings called kugels. Here is a basic recipe. A sweetish apple version follows.

◆   ◆   ◆

2 cups matzo farfel
1 cup diced onions
2 tablespoons shmaltz
4 eggs
Salt
Freshly ground black pepper

Preheat the oven to 350 degrees. Lightly grease an 8-inch square baking pan (or other ovenproof dish with a capacity of 6 cups).

Cover the farfel with 2 cups boiling water and let stand for 5 minutes. Drain well, pressing out as much liquid as possible.

Cook the onions in the shmaltz until soft.

Lightly beat the eggs in a bowl. Add the onions, drained farfel, and salt and pepper and mix well. Transfer the mixture to the prepared pan and bake for 35 to 40 minutes, until the kugel is brown on top and set.
Makes 6 servings.

Matzo Farfel Apple Kugel

2 cups matzo farfel
4 eggs
1/4 cup sugar
1 teaspoon salt
5 tablespoons margarine, melted and cooled
2 apples, peeled, cored, and sliced
1 teaspoon lemon juice
1/4 cup ground walnuts

Preheat the oven to 350 degrees. Lightly grease a 1-quart baking dish with margarine.

Combine the farfel with 2 of the eggs. Place in a heavy skillet and toast over low heat, stirring all the time, until the farfel is golden brown and the pieces are separate.

Beat the remaining 2 eggs with the sugar, salt, and 3 tablespoons margarine. Add the farfel and 1/2 cup of water.

Line the bottom of the prepared baking dish with half of the apple slices and sprinkle with the lemon juice. Add the matzo farfel mixture. Top with the remaining apple slices, sprinkle with the nuts, and pour on the remaining margarine. Bake for 30 minutes. *Makes 6 to 8 servings.*

Potato-Matzo Kugel

2 to 2 1/2 pounds potatoes, peeled
2 onions, peeled
4 eggs, lightly beaten
1 cup matzo meal
1/2 cup vegetable oil, shmaltz, or margarine
Salt
Freshly ground black pepper

Preheat the oven to 400 degrees. Oil the inside of a 2-quart gratin or other baking dish.

Grate the potatoes and onions in a processor in batches, and as each batch is done, place in a strainer set over a bowl. Squeeze as much moisture as you can from the potatoes and onions, then put the vegetables in a mixing bowl. Pour off the liquid in the bowl, being careful to keep the thick starch sticking to the bottom. Add this starch to the potatoes and onions along with the eggs, matzo meal, oil (or shmaltz or margarine), and salt and pepper. Stir well. Turn the mixture into the prepared pan and bake for about 45 minutes, until the kugel is browned and bubbling. *Makes 8 servings.*

KNEIDLACH
MATZO BALLS

*T*hese are nothing more than dumplings made with matzo meal (and, of course, shmaltz). As with all dumplings, there are two schools of thought: you can make them light, or you can make them dense and dangerous to drop on your foot. We opt for lightness.

◆　　　◆　　　◆

4 eggs
1/2 cup water or seltzer
6 tablespoons melted shmaltz
Salt
Freshly ground black pepper
1 cup matzo meal

Beat the eggs until whites and yolks are blended. Stir in the water or seltzer, shmaltz, and salt and pepper. Gradually stir in the matzo meal. Cover and refrigerate for at least 1 hour.

Bring a large quantity of water to a boil. Form the matzo balls with moistened palms, using about 2 tablespoons for each ball. Drop into the boiling water and simmer, covered, for about 30 minutes. Serve in chicken soup (see page 48). *Makes about 16 matzo balls.*

Variation: before stirring in the matzo meal, add 2 teaspoons grated fresh ginger, a few gratings of nutmeg, and 3 tablespoons minced parsley to the egg mixture.

MATZO SCHALET

*T*he word *schalet* derives from Judeo-French and means hot (see page 24). Like its cognate cholent, this dish is meant to be served as a hot component of the Sabbath midday meal on Passover.

◆　　　◆　　　◆

6 tablespoons margarine, melted and cooled
3 matzos
3 eggs
1/2 cup brown sugar
2 cups peeled and chopped apples
1/2 cup chopped walnuts
1/2 cup raisins
1/2 teaspoon cinnamon
1 teaspoon lemon juice

Preheat the oven to 350 degrees. Use a little of the margarine to grease an 8-inch square baking dish or 6-cup ovenproof dish.

Break up the matzos and soak them in warm water for 2 to 3 minutes. Remove from the water and squeeze out as much liquid as possible.

Beat the eggs with the brown sugar for about 10 minutes in a standing mixer or with an electric hand beater, until the mixture is pale beige and has substantially increased in volume. Stir in the squeezed matzos, apples, walnuts, raisins, cinnamon, and lemon juice. Turn the mixture into the prepared baking dish and bake for 25 to 35 minutes, until the top is lightly browned and the schalet is dry. *Makes 8 to 10 servings.*

Matzo Brei

Some people eat matzo brei all year round. They are not watching their cholesterol. Think of this as French toast for Passover (or *pain,* but not *peine, perdu*).

◆   ◆   ◆

3 matzos
4 eggs
Salt
3 tablespoons butter

Break the matzos in half and then in half again. Soak in hot water for 1 to 2 minutes. Remove and, with your hands, squeeze out as much water as you can.

Beat the eggs lightly with salt in a mixing bowl. Add the matzo and mix.

Heat the butter in a heavy skillet and when it starts to turn brown, add the eggs and matzos. Either leave the mixture to set on the bottom and then turn as you would a pancake or stir with a wooden spoon as you would for scrambled eggs. Either way, the matzo brei will be done within 5 minutes, depending on how well done you like your eggs. Serve immediately with jam and/or sour cream. *Makes 2 servings.*

Potato Croquettes

When you tire of matzo and matzoid starch dishes, here is a religiously respectable alternative.

◆   ◆   ◆

2 baking potatoes (about 3/4 pound each)
4 eggs, separated
Salt
Freshly ground black pepper
Oil for frying

Boil the potatoes in their skins until tender. Peel the potatoes and mash them with an old-fashioned potato masher, or put them through a ricer or a food mill.

Add the egg yolks one a time, beating well after each addition until thoroughly incorporated. Season with salt and pepper.

Beat the egg whites until stiff and fold them into the potatoes.

Heat 1/4 inch of oil in a heavy skillet. Drop in the potato mixture by tablespoonfuls and fry on both sides until golden. Add more oil as necessary. Drain the croquettes on paper towels as they are done and serve immediately. *Makes 30 to 35 croquettes.*

Three Passover Pancakes

Matzo Meal and Apple Pancakes

3 eggs, separated
1/2 cup matzo meal
1/2 cup water or milk
1 teaspoon salt
1/2 to 3/4 cup minced peeled apple
Vegetable oil or butter for frying
Cinnamon

Beat the egg yolks until thick and pale in color.

In a small bowl, combine the matzo meal with the water or milk; stir into the beaten yolks.

Beat the egg whites with the salt until stiff. Fold into the yolk mixture. Gently stir in the apple.

Heat 1/4 inch of oil or butter in a heavy skillet. Drop the batter by tablespoonfuls into the hot oil; flatten slightly with the back of the spoon. Fry the pancakes until golden, about 4 minutes; turn and cook for about 3 minutes on the second side. Don't crowd the pan. Add more oil or butter to the skillet as needed. Drain the pancakes on paper towels and sprinkle with cinnamon. Serve with warmed honey, passed separately. *Makes 14 to 18 pancakes.*

Cheese Latkes

4 eggs
1 tablespoon sugar
8 ounces farmer cheese (1 cup)
3 tablespoons butter, melted
1/2 teaspoon vanilla extract
1 tablespoon salt
1/3 to 1/2 cup matzo meal
Vegetable oil, butter, or margarine, for frying
Cinnamon

Beat the eggs and sugar for a few minutes, until pale and increased somewhat in volume. Beat in the farmer cheese. Add the butter, vanilla extract, and salt. Slowly stir in enough matzo meal to make a batter that holds together.

In a heavy skillet, heat 1/4 inch of oil (or butter or margarine). Drop the batter by tablespoonfuls into the hot oil. Flatten the pancakes slightly with the back of a spoon. Fry for 3 to 4 minutes on the first side; flip and fry the second side for about 3 minutes. Don't crowd the pan and add more fat to the skillet as needed. Drain the latkes on paper towels and serve sprinkled with cinnamon. Pass sour cream and/or jam separately. *Makes 18 to 20 latkes.*

CHREMSLACH

6 eggs, separated
1/2 cup sugar
1 teaspoon grated lemon peel
1/2 cup chopped walnuts
1 cup matzo meal
Salt
Oil for frying
3 tablespoons honey

With a whisk, beat the egg yolks with the sugar until the mixture is light yellow and very smooth. Add the lemon peel, walnuts, matzo meal, and salt.

Beat the egg whites until stiff and fold them into the matzo meal mixture.

Heat a thin film of oil in the bottom of a heavy skillet. Melt the honey in the oil and then drop the batter into the skillet by table-spoonful. (Don't crowd the skillet and add more oil as necessary. Regulate the heat so the honey doesn't burn.) Cook for 4 minutes, until bubbles form on the surface of the pancakes or bottom is golden brown. Flip and cook for 2 minutes longer. Drain the chremslach on paper towels and serve. *Makes 20 chremslach.*

NUANT
NUT CANDY

All right, call it walnut brittle. And eat it any time.

1 cup honey
1 tablespoon lemon juice
1 pound walnuts, chopped (3 1/2 cups)

◆   ◆   ◆

Bring the honey and lemon juice to a boil, stirring constantly. Add the nuts and keep stirring until the mixture is thick and rich brown in color. Be careful not to let it burn.

Pour the mixture onto a board moistened with cold water. With the back of a wooden spoon dipped in cold water, smooth the nuts to a thickness of about 1/4 inch. Let cool completely and harden. Break the candy into bite-size pieces and store in a tin. *Makes 1 1/2 pounds.*

The seder ends in a splendor of non-flour sweets—a bowl of nuant (walnut brittle) and a piece of honey sponge cake (page 154)—with a glass of tea.

Two Cakes

Baking cakes with matzo meal, even finely ground cake meal, is a bit of a stunt. The large quantity of eggs in both these cakes is what gives them their extraordinary lightness.

◆　　◆　　◆

Honey Sponge Cake

1/3 cup matzo cake meal

1/3 cup potato starch

1/2 cup sugar

1 teaspoon cinnamon

1 teaspoon ground ginger

Pinch of freshly grated nutmeg

8 eggs, separated

1 egg white

1/4 cup vegetable oil

1 cup honey

Preheat the oven to 325 degrees. Lightly oil a 10-inch tube pan.

Combine the matzo cake meal, potato starch, sugar, cinnamon, ginger, and nutmeg. Make a well in the center and one by one, add the egg yolks, beating well after each addition. Beat in the oil and the honey.

With an electric mixer, beat the 9 egg whites until stiff but not dry. Gently fold the beaten whites into the batter. Turn the mixture into the prepared pan and bake for about 1 hour, until the top of the cake is a rich brown and a skewer inserted in the center tests clean. *Makes 8 to 10 servings.*

Passover Nut Cake

10 eggs, separated
1 cup sugar
2 tablespoons matzo cake meal
1 tablespoon slivovitz (plum brandy)
1/2 pound walnuts, finely ground (scant 1 1/2
*   cups)*

Preheat the oven to 350 degrees. Lightly grease a 9-inch springform pan.

Beat the egg yolks with the sugar until the mixture is pale yellow and thick. Add the cake meal and slivovitz. Slowly beat in the ground nuts.

With an electric mixer, beat the egg whites until stiff but not dry. Gently fold them into the yolk-nut mixture. Turn the batter into the prepared pan and bake for 50 minutes to 1 hour, until the cake has risen substantially and is lightly colored on top. Cool the cake on a rack; as it cools, it will deflate. Remove the sides of the pan. The cake is best served the day it is made. *Makes 6 to 8 servings.*

Breads
and
Pastries

♦   ♦   ♦

Cheesecake (page 168) at home: no glazed
strawberries, no surly waiters, no surly waiters' jokes.

DATE NUT BREAD

1 1/2 cups coarsely chopped dates (12 ounces)

2 teaspoons baking soda

3 tablespoons shortening

1/2 cup sugar

1/4 cup brown sugar

2 eggs

1 teaspoon vanilla extract

2 cups unbleached flour

1 teaspoon salt

1 cup coarsely chopped walnuts or pecans

Preheat the oven to 350 degrees. Lightly grease a 9 × 5 × 3 1/2-inch loaf pan.

Combine the dates and baking soda. Pour 1 cup boiling water over the dates and stir to mix. Let stand for 10 to 15 minutes, until lukewarm.

Cream the shortening with the sugars. Beat in the eggs and the vanilla. Alternately add the flour and salt and the dates and their liquid. When well combined, stir in the chopped nuts.

Pour the batter into the prepared pan and bake for 1 hour to 1 hour and 15 minutes, until the bread tests done. *Makes 1 loaf.*

CHALLAH

*T*his is the braided brioche that graces every traditional Sabbath table. Observant cooks pinch off an olive-size piece of the dough and burn it in the oven while the challah bakes. "Taking challah" symbolizes the tithe given to the priests at the time of the Temple in Jerusalem.

◆   ◆   ◆

1 envelope (1/4 ounce) active dry yeast

2 tablespoons sugar

7 to 8 cups flour

2 teaspoons salt

1/2 cup vegetable oil

3 eggs, lightly beaten

1 cup raisins (for round holiday loaves)

1 egg yolk, lightly beaten with 1 tablespoon
water and a pinch of salt

1/4 cup poppy seeds (optional)

Sprinkle the yeast and 1 teaspoon sugar over 1/4 cup warm (105 degrees) water and stir. Set aside until the yeast is foamy, 5 to 15 minutes.

In a large bowl, combine 5 cups of the flour with the remaining 1 2/3 tablespoons sugar, the salt, oil, and eggs. Mix with a wooden spoon or with the dough hook in a standing electric mixer. Stir in the yeast mixture. Slowly add 2 more cups of flour, up to 1 cup water, and the raisins, if you are using them. Turn the dough out onto a floured board and knead for 10 to 15 minutes, adding up to 1/2 cup more water (using moistened hands) or 1 cup flour. The dough should be supple and soft but not sticky. Form the dough into a ball.

Wipe out and lightly oil the mixing bowl. Place the dough in the bowl, cover with a dish towel, and set aside in a draft-free place to rise. In 1 1/2 to 2 hours, the dough should have doubled in bulk and when you poke it with your finger, the hole created will remain. Turn the dough out onto a board, punch it down, and knead for 2 or 3 minutes. Put the dough back in the bowl, cover with the dish towel, and let rise again. The second rising should take 45 minutes to 1 hour. Test as before.

Punch down the dough and remove a small piece for the mitzvah or good deed of separating the challah (this morsel is to be baked and burned in a traditional gesture toward the priestly tribe, the kohanim). Divide the main part of the dough into 6 equal pieces and roll each piece into a rope about 12 inches long. The ends should be thinner than the centers. Vertically line up three of the ropes in front of you and pinch the top ends together. Start braiding with the rope on the right, bringing it over the middle rope. Turn the left rope over the middle rope and continue in this manner until the full length of each rope has been braided. Pinch the bottom ends together. The braiding should be tight; don't stretch the ropes and don't leave holes as you braid. Repeat with the remaining three ropes to form a second loaf.

For a round loaf, roll half the dough into a tapered rope about 18 inches long. Using the thicker end as the center, coil the remainder around it. Pinch the end tight against the side. Now form a second loaf with the other half of the dough.

Any leftover bits of dough can be rolled and braided and placed on top of the larger loaves, or used as rolls.

Place the loaves on greased cookie sheets, cover with towels, and let rise for 30 minutes. Preheat the oven to 350 degrees.

Brush the egg wash over the breads and sprinkle with the poppy seeds, if you are using them. Bake for 30 to 45 minutes, depending on the sizes of your loaves; they should be golden on top and sound hollow when tapped with your fist. Cool on racks. *Makes 2 loaves.*

MANDELBROT

Almond bread is, for me, the difference between an average and a fine Sunday brunch.

3 cups unbleached flour
1 tablespoon baking powder
1/4 teaspoon salt
4 eggs
1 1/2 cups sugar
1/2 cup vegetable oil
1/2 teaspoon almond extract
1 teaspoon vanilla extract
1 tablespoon grated orange or lemon peel
1/2 to 2 cups whole toasted blanched almonds

Preheat the oven to 350 degrees.

Sift together the flour, baking powder, and salt.

Beat the eggs with the sugar until mixture is thick and pale. Add the oil and extracts. Beat in the sifted dry ingredients and the citrus peel. Fold in the almonds. Add more flour if the dough is too sticky to work with.

Shape the dough into 4 logs, about 2 inches in diameter. Place the rolls on 1 or 2 greased cookie sheets or jellyroll pans and bake for 30 to 45 minutes, until light brown.

Remove the logs and cut each one into 1/2-inch slices. Put the slices back on the cookie sheets, cut side down, and toast in the oven for 5 minutes; turn each slice and toast for 5 minutes more. Cool on a rack and store in an airtight container. *Makes about 4 dozen.*

Mandelbrot: gently sweet, brittle almond bread.

OVERLEAF: *Kosher ambrosia. Clockwise from left: teiglach, rugelach (page 164), kichlach (page 167), and schnecken (page 166).*

MANDELTORTE
ALMOND CAKE

For Middle European bakers, a torte is a cake where ground nuts supplant flour as the main solid ingredient. This one is typical. And delicious.

◆   ◆   ◆

5 eggs, separated
1/2 cup sugar
1/3 cup plus 2 tablespoons flour
5 ounces (2/3 cup) blanched almonds, toasted in a 300-degree oven and ground in a clean coffee grinder or pounded in a mortar (scant 1 1/4 cups)
2 tablespoons butter, melted and cooled
1/4 teaspoon vanilla extract
Salt
1/2 cup apricot preserves

Preheat the oven to 350 degrees. Butter and flour a 9 x 1 1/4-inch round cake pan.

Beat the egg yolks with 1/4 cup sugar until light in color, smooth, and very thick, about 10 minutes at high speed in a standing mixer. Add the flour, 3/4 cup ground almonds, the butter, and the vanilla. Mix gently but well.

Beat the egg whites with a pinch of salt. When they start to mount, add the remaining 1/4 cup sugar and beat until stiff. Gently fold the whites into the batter and pour into the prepared cake pan. Smooth the top and bake for 30 minutes, until the top is lightly colored and the cake tests done in the center. Cool in the pan for 10 minutes. Turn out onto a rack and cool completely.

Heat the apricot preserves until spreadable. Slice the cake in half horizontally. Put the bottom half on a flat cake plate and spread with the preserves. Carefully replace the top half. Spread the top and sides of the cake with the preserves and sprinkle with the remaining 1/2 cup ground almonds. *Makes 6 to 8 servings.*

Rugelach I

Rugelach are crescent-shaped sweet pastries made with a dough containing sour cream. They are stuffed with nuts and raisins, as in this recipe, or with preserves, as in the next recipe. Cinnamon is the spice that links both kinds.

◆　　◆　　◆

1 pound margarine, softened
2 cups sour cream
4 cups unbleached flour
1 tablespoon cinnamon
5 tablespoons sugar
1 1/2 cups chopped toasted almonds or walnuts
1 cup raisins
8 tablespoons (1 stick) butter, melted

Beat together the margarine, sour cream, and flour until well combined. Form the dough into a ball, wrap in wax paper, and refrigerate overnight.

Preheat the oven to 350 degrees. Grease 2 cookie sheets.

In a small bowl, combine the cinnamon, sugar, nuts, and raisins.

Divide the dough into 6 equal pieces. On a lightly floured board, roll out one piece at a time to form a circle about 6 inches in diameter and about 1/4 inch thick. Brush each circle with melted butter and sprinkle with the sugar-nut-raisin mixture. Cut each circle into 8 pie-shape wedges and roll up, starting with the wide outer edge. Pinch closed and place on the greased cookie sheets. Bake for about 30 minutes, until the rugelach are lightly browned. *Makes about 4 dozen.*

Rugelach II

8 tablespoons (1 stick) butter, at room temperature
4 ounces cream cheese, at room temperature
1/2 cup sour cream
1 egg
1/4 teaspoon salt
2 1/2 to 3 cups unbleached flour
1/2 cup apricot preserves
1 cup chopped walnuts
1/2 cup brown sugar
1/2 cup raisins
Cinnamon

Cream together the butter and cream cheese. Beat in the sour cream and the egg, followed by the salt and 2 1/2 cups flour. The dough should be smooth and elastic; add up to 1/2 cup more flour, if necessary, to give it body. Form the dough into a ball, wrap in wax paper, and refrigerate for at least 4 hours.

Preheat the oven to 350 degrees. Grease 2 cookie sheets.

Divide the dough into four equal pieces. Roll each piece into a circle 1/8 inch thick on a floured board with a floured rolling pin.

Heat the apricot preserves until spreadable. Brush the circles of dough with the preserves. Sprinkle on the nuts, sugar, and raisins, and then dust lightly with cinnamon. Cut the circles into pie-shape wedges about 3 inches at the base. Roll the rugelach from the base up to the point to form into crescents, and pinch closed. Place the rugelach on the cookie sheets and bake for 30 to 40 minutes, until lightly browned. *Makes about 40 rugelach.*

TEIGLACH

The name means something like "doughies." Teiglach in fact consists of small balls of dough glazed with a honey mixture, covered with chopped nuts, and formed into a pyramid. A sweet tooth is required for full enjoyment on Rosh Hashanah, the Jewish New Year, when teiglach is served.

◆　　　◆　　　◆

1 1/2 to 2 cups unbleached flour
1 teaspoon baking powder
Pinch of salt
3 tablespoons vegetable oil
3 eggs
1 1/2 cups (1 pound) flavorful honey
1/2 cup dark brown sugar
1 teaspoon ground ginger
1/2 teaspoon grated nutmeg
1 teaspoon chopped lemon peel
2 cups coarsely chopped nuts (about 1/2
    pound): walnuts, pecans, blanched almonds,
    and hazelnuts

Preheat the oven to 350 degrees. Grease a large cookie sheet.

Sift 1 1/2 cups flour with the baking powder and salt. Add the vegetable oil and the eggs. Mix with a wooden spoon or with the paddle of a standing electric mixer. Add more flour if necessary to make a smooth, elastic dough.

Roll small pieces of the dough into ropes about 1/2 inch thick. Cut the ropes into 1/2-inch pieces. Roll each piece in the palm of your hand to make it round and place on the cookie sheet. You should have between 60 and 70 balls; the balls should be roughly the same size and shape so they cook evenly. Bake in 2 or 3 batches for 15 to 20 minutes, just until very lightly browned. Remove from the oven and let cool for 5 to 10 minutes.

Combine the honey, brown sugar, ginger, nutmeg, and lemon peel in a large enameled saucepan. Stir with a wooden spoon and break up any lumps in the brown sugar. Bring to a boil and immediately lower the heat. Simmer for 10 minutes. Add the warm dough balls and simmer for another 10 minutes, stirring with a wooden spoon. Add the chopped nuts and simmer, stirring, for a final 10 minutes.

Let the mixture cool in the pan for 10 to 15 minutes, stirring occasionally. Reoil the cookie sheet and turn the mixture out onto it. Let stand until cool enough to handle.

Moisten your hands with cold water and form the mixture into a pyramid. This is best done on a doily placed on a serving plate. If you plan to keep the teiglach for a few days, place it in an airtight tin. *Makes about 2 pounds.*

KICHLACH

*T*hese cookies are traditionally served on the Sabbath.

◆　　◆　　◆

3 eggs, at room temperature
2 tablespoons sugar
1/2 cup vegetable oil
Salt
1 cup unbleached flour

In a standing electric mixer, beat the eggs for several minutes until light and substantially increased in volume. Add 1 tablespoon sugar, the oil, and a pinch of salt. Beat for a moment or two and then add the flour. Beat until combined.

Preheat the oven to 325 degrees. Grease 2 cookie sheets.

Drop the dough onto the cookie sheets by teaspoonfuls, about 2 or 3 inches apart. Sprinkle the remaining tablespoon sugar over the cookies and bake for 20 to 30 minutes, until lightly browned and puffed. *Makes about 50 cookies.*

Variations: to make mohn kichlach, add 2 to 3 tablespoons poppy seeds to the dough with the sugar.

In Israel, kichlach are sometimes made with sesame seeds. Sprinkle on 1 to 2 tablespoons sesame seeds along with the final tablespoon of sugar just before baking.

SCHNECKEN

*S*chnecken means snails. These pastries are formed from a yeast dough rolled around a filling of currants, cinnamon, and nuts, and then sliced into coiled-up little toothsome "snails."

◆　　◆　　◆

DOUGH

2 envelopes (1/4-ounce each) active dry yeast
1/4 cup sugar
1/4 cup lukewarm milk
8 tablespoons (1 stick) butter, melted and cooled
1/2 cup sour cream
1/2 teaspoon lemon juice
3 cups flour
2 egg yolks, lightly beaten

FILLING

1 cup brown sugar
1/2 pound (2 sticks) butter, at room temperature
1 teaspoon cinnamon
3/4 cup currants
1 1/2 cups finely chopped walnuts

Sprinkle the yeast over 1/4 cup warm water (105 degrees). Add a pinch of sugar and stir. Set aside for 5 to 10 minutes, until the mixture is foamy.

Combine the remaining sugar with the milk, butter, sour cream, and lemon juice in a large bowl. Stir in the yeast mixture. Gradually stir in the flour. Work in the egg yolks. The dough should be moist and workable, but not sticky.

Turn the dough out onto a floured board and knead for 15 minutes, or until smooth. Put the dough in a large buttered bowl, cover, and refrigerate for at least 4 hours, or up to 3 days. The dough should double in bulk. When ready to use, stir the dough with a wooden spoon to deflate it.

For the filling, cream 1/2 cup of the brown sugar with 1 stick of the butter. Use a small amount of this mixture to grease the bottoms and sides of 4 muffin tins (see note). Reserve the rest.

Melt the remaining stick of butter and let cool.

In a small bowl, combine the remaining 1/2 cup brown sugar with the cinnamon, currants, and walnuts and combine with reserved filling mixture.

Divide the dough into 4 pieces. With a floured rolling pin, roll each piece of dough on a floured board into a rectangle between 1/8 and 1/4 inch thick. Brush each rectangle with some of the melted butter and sprinkle with the sugar-nut mixture. Tightly roll up lengthwise, like a jellyroll. Slice the roll into pieces about 1 inch wide, or large enough to fill the muffin cups about half full, with the slice placed cut side down. Cover loosely with a kitchen towel and let rise for about 1 hour, until the dough looks puffy.

Preheat the oven to 350 degrees.

Brush the tops of the shnecken with a little melted butter and bake for 20 minutes or until rich brown in color. Invert the muffin tin over a cookie sheet the moment you take it out of the oven. Let stand for a few seconds, then lift the tin and let the shnecken fall out gently. *Makes 3 to 4 dozen shnecken.*

Note: four muffin tins are ideal but not necessary. If you have fewer tins, slice all the dough and let the extra slices rise on a board or on a greased cookie sheet, under a towel. The schnecken can be baked in batches in the tins you have, or on the cookie sheet.

CHEESECAKE

*H*ere is a rich and satisfying example of the ultimate milchik dessert. To fancy it up with strawberries or cherries, as delicatessens do, would spoil the purity of the cake.

◆　　　◆　　　◆

COOKIE CRUST

1 cup flour

1/4 cup sugar

1 teaspoon grated lemon peel

8 tablespoons (1 stick) cold unsalted butter, cut into pieces

1 egg yolk

FILLING

8 ounces cream cheese, at room temperature

1 cup sour cream

2 eggs

1/4 cup sugar

1/2 teaspoon vanilla extract

1/2 teaspoon grated lemon peel

TOPPING

1 cup sour cream

1 tablespoon sugar

1 teaspoon grated lemon peel

1/2 teaspoon lemon juice

To make the crust, combine the flour, sugar, lemon peel, butter, and egg yolk in the bowl of a standing mixer. Beat until the ingredients are well combined and form a ball. Alternatively, mix the ingredients with a wooden spoon and your fingers. Wrap the dough in wax paper and refrigerate for 1 to 2 hours. Remove from refrigerator.

Preheat the oven to 400 degrees.

Pat the dough as evenly as you can into a 9-inch springform pan, spreading it halfway up the sides. Bake for 10 minutes, until the edges of crust just begin to color. Cool for 20 to 40 minutes. Lower the oven temperature to 375 degrees.

To make the filling, beat together the cream cheese and sour cream. Add the eggs, sugar, vanilla, and lemon peel. Combine well. Pour the filling into the cooled crust and bake for 25 to 35 minutes, until firm. Remove and let cool for 30 minutes. Raise the oven temperature to 475 degrees.

Beat the topping ingredients with a whisk. Carefully spread the mixture over the cheesecake and bake for 5 to 8 minutes, until set and firm. Cool and chill before serving. *Makes 10 to 12 servings.*

APPLE MERINGUE

*T*his is an elegant survival from the nineteenth century: stewed apples baked under a layer of meringue.

◆　　◆　　◆

3 pounds tart apples, peeled, cored, and sliced
　(about 7 cups)
1/2 cup sugar
1/2 teaspoon cinnamon
1 teaspoon grated lemon peel
1 teaspoon lemon juice
1/4 cup apple cider or water
1 cup chopped walnuts
3 egg whites
Salt

Preheat the oven to 300 degrees.

Mix the apples with 1/4 cup sugar, the cinnamon, lemon peel, lemon juice, cider or water, and walnuts. Place the mixture in a flameproof round or oval gratin dish. Gently stew over low heat for about 10 minutes. Some of the apple slices should remain whole while others will have disintegrated. If the apples give off a lot of liquid, drain some off before continuing.

Beat the egg whites with a pinch of salt. When they start to mount, add the remaining 1/4 cup sugar and beat until stiff. Mound the meringue over the apples and bake for about 30 minutes, until the meringue is lightly browned. Serve warm or at room temperature. *Makes 6 to 8 servings.*

APPLE STRUDEL

Store-bought frozen strudel or phyllo dough is tricky to use but becomes at least quite manageable, if not easy, with experience. On your first try, you may ruin more than you use, but don't give up. If you keep the unused dough damp and cool, you should have few problems. Before you start assembling the strudel, have the filling prepared, the butter melted, the bread crumbs handy, and the dough defrosted.

◆   ◆   ◆

2 pounds tart apples, peeled, cored, and thinly
    sliced (4 to 5 cups)
1 cup golden raisins
1 teaspoon cinnamon
Nutmeg
1 cup coarsely chopped walnuts
1 tablespoon lemon juice
3 tablespoons grated lemon peel
1/2 to 3/4 cup sugar
8 tablespoons (1 stick) unsalted butter or
    margarine, melted and cooled
1 pound frozen strudel leaves or phyllo dough,
    defrosted overnight in the refrigerator
1/2 cup plain dry bread crumbs, lightly toasted

Put the apple slices in a large mixing bowl and add the raisins, cinnamon, a few gratings of nutmeg, the walnuts, lemon juice, lemon peel, and sugar to taste. Mix together with a wooden spoon and set aside.

Preheat the oven to 375 degrees. Brush some melted butter or margarine on a large cookie sheet.

Place a damp teatowel on a work surface and unroll the dough leaves onto another damp towel right next to the first. Gently remove one layer of dough and place on the damp towel. Roll up the remaining dough in its damp towel. Brush the single layer of dough with melted butter or margarine and sprinkle with bread crumbs. Unroll the reserved dough, place a second layer on top of the buttered layer, brush with butter or margarine, and sprinkle with bread crumbs. Continue layering until 4 or 5 layers have been prepared. Spread one third of the apple filling over the bottom third of the dough, leaving a 1-inch margin on the bottom and two sides. With the help of the damp towel, roll up the strudel from the short end, tucking in the sides. Place on the prepared cookie sheet, seam side down. Repeat the process to make two more strudels.

Brush the top of each strudel with melted butter and bake for 30 to 45 minutes, until the tops are brown and the strudels are crisp. Serve warm or at room temperature, dusted with confectioners' sugar. *Makes three 10 × 5 inch strudels.*

Apple strudel, ready to roll.

POPPY SEED CAKE

4 tablespoons butter
1/2 cup sugar
3 eggs, separated
1 teaspoon vanilla extract
1 1/2 cups flour
1 teaspoon baking powder
1/4 teaspoon salt
1 cup brown sugar, coarsely sieved
1 cup poppy seeds (about 5 ounces)

Preheat the oven to 350 degrees. Lightly grease two 8-inch square baking pans.

Cream together the butter and sugar. Add the egg yolks and mix well. Beat in the vanilla. Add the flour and baking powder. Mix well. Divide the somewhat crumbly batter between the 2 baking pans and smooth the tops.

Beat the egg whites with the salt. When they start to mount, gradually add the brown sugar. Beat until stiff. Fold in the poppy seeds. Spread the egg-white mixture over the batter in the pans. Bake for 30 minutes. Cool in the pans. Carefully turn out on a rack and invert onto 2 cake plates. Serve at room temperature. *Each cake serves 6 to 8.*

HONEY CAKE

4 eggs
1 cup sugar
2 tablespoons vegetable oil
1 cup honey
1/2 cup warm coffee
3 cups unbleached flour
1 teaspoon baking powder
1 teaspoon baking soda
1/4 teaspoon ground cloves
1/2 teaspoon cinnamon
A few gratings of nutmeg
1/2 cup chopped walnuts
1/2 cup raisins

Preheat the oven to 350 degrees. Oil a 9-inch tube pan or two 9 × 5-inch loaf pans.

Beat the eggs with the sugar until they are very pale. Add the vegetable oil.

Dilute the honey with the warm coffee.

Sift together the flour, baking powder, baking soda, cloves, cinnamon, and nutmeg. Add to the eggs, alternating with the honey, beginning and ending with the flour mixture and beating well after each addition. Stir in the nuts and raisins.

Turn the batter into the prepared pans and bake for 50 minutes to 1 hour, until the top is brown and the cake tests done. Cool on a rack and remove from the pans. *Makes 10 to 12 servings.*

Babka

*T*his is a yeast dough flavored with lemon peel and raisins and baked in a high mold. High pleasure at high tea or dessert any time.

◆　　　◆　　　◆

1 envelope (1/4 ounce) active dry yeast
1/2 cup sugar
12 tablespoons (1 1/2 sticks) unsalted butter, at room temperature
8 egg yolks
1 cup milk
3 cups cake flour
1/2 teaspoon salt
1 1/2 tablespoons grated lemon peel
1 cup raisins

Sprinkle the yeast over 1/4 cup warm water (105 degrees). Add 1 teaspoon sugar and stir to mix. Let stand for 10 minutes. The mixture will have increased in volume and look foamy and bubbly.

In the bowl of a standing electric mixer, beat the butter with the remaining sugar until smooth. Add the egg yolks, beating and incorporating each one before adding the next. The mixture should be smooth and pale.

Warm the milk to 110 degrees.

Add 1 1/2 cups of the flour to the yolks along with the yeast mixture and combine. Add the remaining flour alternately with the warm milk, beating as you do so.

If your machine has a dough hook, insert it and knead for 5 minutes. If it doesn't, continue with the beater or use your hands. Stir in the salt, lemon peel, and raisins.

Butter a 10-cup kugelhopf mold or fluted tube pan and pour in the batter. Smooth the top of the dough with a wooden spoon. Cover the mold with a kitchen towel and let rise for about 2 hours, until the dough reaches close to the top of the pan.

Toward the end of the rising, preheat the oven to 400 degrees. When the babka batter has fully risen in the mold, place in the oven and immediately lower the temperature to 350 degrees. Bake for 30 to 35 minutes. The top should be brown and the cake should test clean. Remove from the oven and let stand in the pan for 10 to 15 minutes. Then invert the babka onto a rack and let cool. *Makes 8 to 12 servings.*

OVERLEAF: *Hamantaschen (page 176): edible tricorns for Purim. He who takes Haman's purse eats lekvar (or poppy seeds).*

HAMANTASCHEN

*P*urim is a spring holiday commemorating the heroic actions of Esther, Jewish Queen of Persia, who intervened and prevented the villainous courtier Haman from massacring her people. *Hamantaschen* literally means Haman's pockets. I was taught that these triangular pastries, which are the holiday's traditional food, were inspired by Haman's three-cornered hat. They are, in any case, pockets of pastry usually stuffed either with a sweet poppy seed mixture or with the dark prune butter sold as lekvar.

◆   ◆   ◆

Cookie Dough

2 cups unbleached flour

1 teaspoon baking powder

Pinch of salt

1/2 cup sugar

8 tablespoons (1 stick) cold butter, cut into
    small pieces

2 eggs, lightly beaten

1 tablespoon grated lemon peel

Sift the flour, baking powder, salt, and sugar into a large bowl. Work in the butter using a pastry blender or two forks, one held in each hand. Add the eggs, mixing in with the pastry blender. Add the lemon peel. Form the dough into a ball and wrap in wax paper. Refrigerate for at least 1 hour.

Yeast Dough

1 envelope (1/4 ounce) active dry yeast

1/2 cup sugar

4 to 5 cups unbleached flour

1/2 cup milk

Pinch of salt

2 eggs

8 tablespoons (1 stick) butter or margarine,
    melted and cooled

Sprinkle the yeast over 1/4 cup lukewarm (105 degrees) water; add a pinch of sugar. Set aside until foamy.

Put 2 cups flour in a large bowl and add the yeast, milk, salt, and the remaining sugar. Beat in the eggs, one at a time. Add the butter or margarine and only enough of the remaining flour to produce a dough that is moist and pliable. Knead for 5 minutes. Form the dough into a ball and place in a large greased bowl. Cover with a dish towel and set aside to rise, 1 to 1 1/2 hours until doubled in bulk.

Mohn (Poppy Seed) Filling

1 cup poppy seeds
1/2 cup honey
1/2 cup milk
1 tablespoon lemon juice
2 teaspoons grated lemon peel
1/2 cup raisins

Combine the poppy seeds, honey, and milk in a small saucepan. Simmer for about 10 minutes, stirring constantly; the mixture should thicken. Stir in the lemon juice, lemon peel, and raisins. Set aside to cool.

Prune Filling

1 pound unsweetened pitted prunes, chopped
  (about 3 cups)
1 tablespoon lemon juice
1/2 cup honey
3/4 cup chopped walnuts (optional)

Cover the prunes with 1 cup water in a small saucepan. Bring to a boil, cover, and simmer for 30 minutes to 1 hour, until tender. Add the lemon juice and honey and simmer slowly for about 10 minutes. Stir in the nuts, if you are using them, and let the filling cool.

Lekvar Filling

1/2 pound lekvar (a commercially available
  prune butter)
1 tablespoon lemon juice
1 tablespoon grated lemon peel
1 tablespoon honey
1 cup chopped walnuts (optional)

Combine all the ingredients.
   Note: all the fillings can be made in advance and stored, covered, in the refrigerator.

Assembly

1 recipe dough
1 recipe filling
1 egg, beaten with 1 tablespoon water

Preheat the oven to 350 degrees.
   Divide whichever dough you choose into portions you can easily roll out. On a floured board, roll out the dough to a thickness of 1/8 to 1/4 inch. The cookie dough rolls out best if placed between 2 sheets of wax paper.
   Cut the dough into 3- to 4-inch circles, using the top of a glass or a cookie cutter. Fill each circle with a heaping teaspoon of filling and pinch the dough around it into a triangular shape. Brush the dough with the egg wash and bake on a greased cookie sheet for 20 to 30 minutes; the cookie dough will bake faster than the yeast dough. When the cookies are done, they will look done—appealingly brown. Taste one if you are in doubt. *Makes about 30 hamantaschen.*

Jellyroll

1 tablespoon butter or margarine
4 eggs, at room temperature
3/4 teaspoon baking powder
Pinch of salt
3/4 cup sugar
1 teaspoon vanilla extract
3/4 cup unbleached flour
1/2 to 3/4 cup jelly
2 tablespoons confectioners' sugar

Preheat the oven to 400 degrees.

Line a 17 x 11 x 1-inch jellyroll pan with aluminum foil. Put the butter or margarine in the pan and melt in the oven. Spread evenly over the foil with a brush.

Put the eggs, baking powder, and salt in the bowl of a standing electric mixer and beat at high speed for 5 minutes, until the mixture is pale and fluffy. Gradually add the sugar and beat for 10 more minutes. The mixture should be very thick and very pale yellow.

Remove the bowl from the stand and add the vanilla. Sift in the flour. Beat again, slowly, just long enough to combine the ingredients. Pour the batter into the prepared pan and even out with a spatula. Bake for 12 to 15 minutes, until the top is springy and lightly colored.

While the cake is baking, heat the jelly in a small pan.

When the cake is done, sprinkle the top with the confectioners' sugar. Cover the cake with a clean kitchen towel and a cookie sheet. Invert the cake onto the cookie sheet and remove the foil. If any edges are brown, cut them off. Brush the warm jelly evenly over the cake and, picking up the short end of the towel nearest you, raise it and roll the cake up by letting it roll forward off the towel and onto itself. Place seam side down on a platter and serve at room temperature. *Makes about ten 1-inch slices.*

Sour Cream Coffeecake

1/2 cup brown sugar
1/2 tablespoon cinnamon
1/2 to 3/4 cup chopped walnuts
2 cups unbleached flour
1 teaspoon baking powder
1 teaspoon baking soda
Salt
8 tablespoons (1 stick) butter, at room temperature
1 cup sugar
2 eggs, separated
1 cup sour cream

Preheat the oven to 350 degrees. Butter the bottom and sides of a 9- to 10-inch spring-form pan.

Combine the brown sugar, cinnamon, and nuts in a small bowl and set aside.

Sift together the flour, baking powder, baking soda, and a pinch of salt.

Cream together the butter and sugar. Beat in the egg yolks and sour cream.

Beat the egg whites until soft peaks form.

Add the dry ingredients to the creamed mixture and mix well. Fold in the egg whites.

Spread half the batter on the bottom of the prepared pan and sprinkle with half the brown sugar mixture. Cover with the remaining batter and sprinkle with the remaining brown sugar mixture. Bake for about 45 minutes, until a tester inserted near the center comes out clean. *Makes 6 to 8 servings.*

Sour cream coffeecake.

Yeast Coffeecake Dough

*T*his basic dough is the basis for several coffee cakes: plain, filled, and rolled. The variations follow.

◆　　　◆　　　◆

3 envelopes (1/4-ounce each) active dry yeast
1/2 cup sugar
1/2 pound (2 sticks) butter, at room
　temperature
Salt
1 teaspoon finely grated lemon peel
3 eggs
1 egg yolk
1 cup milk, scalded and cooled to tepid
1 teaspoon vanilla extract
5 to 6 cups unbleached flour

Sprinkle the yeast over 1/2 cup warm water (105 degrees) in a wide-mouthed measuring cup. Add a pinch of sugar. Stir and set aside for 5 to 15 minutes, until the yeast is foamy.

Cream the butter with the remaining sugar until light in color, thick, and smooth. Add a pinch of salt and the lemon peel, whole eggs, egg yolk, milk, vanilla, and yeast. Beat to combine thoroughly.

Add 3 cups of flour, beating with a wooden spoon until smooth. Add 2 more cups of flour, one at a time, beating well to combine. The dough should be moist and easy to work with, but not sticky. Add more flour if necessary. Turn the dough out onto a floured board and knead for about 15 minutes, until it is elastic and shiny and picks itself up from the board. Turn the dough into a large, straight-sided, lightly oiled bowl. Cover with a wet dish towel and let rise until doubled in bulk; this will take anywhere from 45 minutes to 1 1/2 hours.

Punch the dough down, re-cover, and let rise again until doubled in bulk, 30 minutes to 1 hour longer.

Remove the dough from the bowl, turn it out onto a floured board, and knead lightly before using in one of the following ways.

Apple Coffeecake

1 recipe yeast coffeecake dough (see left)
4 tablespoons butter, melted
2 cups coarsely chopped peeled apples
1 teaspoon cinnamon
2 tablespoons sugar
1/2 cup raisins
1/2 cup chopped walnuts
1 egg, lightly beaten with 1 tablespoon milk

Divide the dough in half and roll each piece into a rectangle 1/8 to 1/4 inch thick. Brush the dough with melted butter.

Cover each rectangle with half the apples, cinnamon, sugar, raisins, and walnuts and roll up like a jellyroll, from the long side. Place each roll seam side down on a lightly buttered jellyroll pan. Brush with melted butter, cover with dish towels, and set aside for about 30 minutes, until risen.

Preheat the oven to 350 degrees.

Brush the tops of the rolls with the egg wash and bake for about 45 minutes, until golden brown. During baking, the rolls will expand and new surfaces will appear; brush these with the egg wash. Cool on racks. Serve in thin slices. *Makes 18 servings.*

STREUSEL COFFEECAKE

1 recipe yeast coffeecake dough (see opposite)
5 tablespoons butter, melted
1/2 cup sugar
1/2 cup finely chopped walnuts (optional)
1 cup flour
1 tablespoon cinnamon

Pat the dough into a 9 x 13-inch baking pan or a 10-inch springform pan. Brush the top with melted butter.

Combine the remaining butter with the other ingredients and sprinkle over the top of the dough. Cover and let rise for about 30 minutes.

Preheat the oven to 350 degrees.

Bake the coffeecake for about 45 minutes, until it tests clean with a skewer and the crumbs are temptingly brown. *Makes 12 servings.*

Note: more butter in the streusel will make for larger crumbs; more flour will yield finer crumbs.

CINNAMON COFFEECAKE

2 tablespoons butter, melted
1 recipe yeast coffeecake dough (see opposite)
1/2 cup sugar
1/2 tablespoon cinnamon

Brush a 9x13-inch baking pan or a 10-inch springform pan with melted butter. Then pat in the yeast dough.

Combine the sugar and cinnamon and sprinkle over the dough. Cover with a dish towel and let rise for 30 minutes.

Preheat the oven to 350 degrees.

Bake the cake for 45 minutes, until it tests clean with a skewer and the top is golden brown. *Makes 12 servings.*

Egg Cream

T his is the drink to have when you're having more than one traditional Jewish dessert. Egg cream sounds rich, but it isn't. Well, not very rich. Think of it as a chocolate ice cream soda without the ice cream.

In the category of deceptively named items, it is the Jewish answer to the Holy Roman Empire and the English horn. As the former was neither holy, Roman, nor an empire (Voltaire), and the latter is neither English nor a horn (George Bernard Shaw), so the egg cream contains neither egg nor cream (Zero Mostel).

Don't ask how this folkloric beverage of the New York streets got its grandiloquent name. Don't ask because you'd be wasting your time. If I knew and I told you, would anyone trust me with a secret anymore?

You want to know if it's all right to add an egg and some cream? It's a free country, isn't it? But don't be a shlemiel. Make it our way. You'll live longer. Go on. Have another.

3 ounces milk

8 ounces seltzer

2 ounces chocolate syrup

Pour the milk into a glass. Spritz in the seltzer. Spoon in the syrup and combine with vigorous wrist action.

An equally accurate system of measurement is your eye: in a 16-ounce glass that measures 5 inches high, pour in 1 inch of milk; spritz in seltzer until foam reaches the top of the glass; spoon in enough chocolate syrup to achieve a nice, rich brown color. *Makes 1 serving.*

CONVERSION CHART

LIQUID MEASURES

Fluid ounces	U.S. measures	Imperial measures	Milliliters	Fluid ounces	U.S. measures	Imperial measures	Milliliters
	1 tsp	1 tsp	5	25		1¼ pints	700
¼	2 tsp	1 dessertspoon	7	27	3½ cups		750
½	1 tbs	1 tbs	15	30	3¾ cups	1½ pints	840
1	2 tbs	2 tbs	28	32	4 cups		900
2	¼ cup	4 tbs	56		or 2 pints		
4	½ cup		110		or 1 quart		
	or ¼ pint			35		1¾ pints	980
5		¼ pint or 1 gill	140	36	4½ cups		1000 or
6	¾ cup		170				1 liter
8	1 cup		225	40	5 cups or	2 pints	1120
	or ½ pint				2½ pints	or 1 quart	
9			250 or	48	6 cups		1350
			¼ liter		or 3 pints		
10	1¼ cups	½ pint	280	50		2½ pints	1400
12	1½ cups		240	60	7½ cups	3 pints	1680
	or ¾ pint			64	8 cups or 4 pints		1800
15		¾ pint	420		or 2 quarts		
16	2 cups or 1 pint		450	72	9 cups		2000 or
18	2¼ cups		500 or				2 liters
			½ liter	80	10 cups or	4 pints	2250
20	2½ cups	1 pint	560		5 pints		
24	3 cups		675	96	12 cups		2700
	or 1½ pints				or 3 quarts		
				100		5 pints	2800

SOLID MEASURES

U.S. and Imperial measures		Metric measures		U.S. and Imperial measures		Metric measures	
Ounces	Pounds	Grams	Kilos	Ounces	Pounds	Grams	Kilos
1		28		27		750	¾
2		56		28	1¾	780	
3½		100		32	2	900	
4	¼	112		36	2¼	1000	1
5		140		40	2½	1100	
6		168		48	3	1350	
8	½	225		54		1500	1½
9		250	¼	64	4	1800	
12	¾	340		72	4½	2000	2
16	1	450		80	5	2250	2¼
18		500	½	90		2500	2½
20	1¼	560		100	6	2800	2¾
24	1½	675					

OVEN TEMPERATURE EQUIVALENTS

FAHRENHEIT	GAS MARK	CELSIUS	HEAT OF OVEN	FAHRENHEIT	GAS MARK	CELSIUS	HEAT OF OVEN
225	¼	107	VERY COOL	375	5	190	FAIRLY HOT
250	½	121	VERY COOL	400	6	204	FAIRLY HOT
275	1	135	COOL	425	7	218	HOT
300	2	148	COOL	450	8	232	VERY HOT
325	3	163	MODERATE	475	9	246	VERY HOT
350	4	177	MODERATE				

TERMINOLOGY EQUIVALENTS

U.S.	BRITISH	U.S.	BRITISH
ZUCCHINI	COURGETTE	BROIL	GRILL
SUGAR, GRANULATED SUGAR	CASTOR SUGAR	SKILLET	FRYING PAN
POWDERED SUGAR	ICING SUGAR	BROILER	GRILL

INDEX

Pages in *italic* contain illustrations

PHOTO CREDITS

Food stylist: Rick Ellis
Prop stylists: Judy Singer
Francesca Bacon
Backdrop artist: Joy Nagy

Page 2: Candlesticks, silverware, dinner
plate, platter, and serving dish courtesy
Cardels, New York, NY.

Page 34: Glasses and round silver dish
courtesy Cardels, New York, NY.

Page 54: Plates and silverware courtesy
Cardels, New York, NY.

Page 75: Glass courtesy Cardels, New
York, NY.

Page 125: Plate courtesy Contemporary
Porcelain. Cutlery courtesy Sasaki.

Page 128: Dishes courtesy Contemporary
Porcelain. Glass courtesy Sasaki.

Page 156: Cake plate, cup, and saucer
courtesy Contemporary Porcelain.
Coffeepot courtesy Swid Powell.

ACKNOWLEDGEMENTS

All members of my immediate family have earned my gratitude for feeding me and my curiosity over the years, but most especially my mother, Josephine Sokolov; my grandmother the late Mary Sokolov; and my aunts, the late Bertha Kaminsky and Bertha Sokolov. I join Susan Friedland in thanking her mother Bertha Grossman and her aunt Mary Friedland for their nurturing presence and for their long memories.

Three men have provided important insights into Jewish food traditions, perhaps without directly intending it: Richard B. Stone, Ben-Zion Gold, and I. B. Singer. Susan Spectorsky directed me to valuable sources in the world of Judeo-Arabic studies. Alan Ternes and Carol Breslin at *Natural History* magazine gave my thoughts on cholent their first home. Andrew Stewart provided this one and made Roy Finamore its able balabos.

Designed by Joseph Rutt

Composed in Goudy Old Style
by Graphic Arts Composition, Inc.,
Philadelphia, Pennsylvania.

Printed and bound
by Toppan Printing Company, Ltd.,
Tokyo, Japan.